FASCINATING CITIES
BERLIN

Schloss Charlottenburg, Berlin's largest and most beautiful palace, was built at the end of the 17th century in the Italian baroque style for the Electress and future Queen Sophie Charlotte.

Caricature kisses between despots: This political mural was painted on one of few remaining sections of the Berlin Wall, which for twenty-eight years (until 1989) divided not only the city but the entire world.

ABOUT THIS BOOK

Since Berlin was once again made the capital of Germany, millions of people have visited the city every year. They walk for miles, from the Reichstag through the Brandenburg Gate, down the Unter den Linden "construction site", across the greenery of the Tiergarten to Potsdamer Platz, and into the new world under the canopy roof on Kollwitzplatz and in the Kastanienallee to search for the myth of Prenzlauer Berg. One million of these people actually stayed after the fall of the Wall in 1989, and exactly the same number moved away, out into the green environs beyond the city limits, away from the endless building sites and the constant "newness" of the city – but some of them return a few years later.

What exactly makes this city so fascinating? This book will attempt to answer that question by juxtaposing the historic with the modern, the traditional with the cutting edge, the glitzy city with the more modest *kiez* (neighborhoods), where Berliners live, unimpressed by and separated from the hordes of tourists. Berlin is a poor city. After World War II and the construction of the Wall, many companies left the city for good. There are not enough jobs. But Berlin is also a rich city that gives young people from around the world the space to realize their dreams and inspire one another.

Berlin is not the rubble heap many envision. It is a history book that tells the story of an entire nation. The short but informative captions accompanying the images in this book tell of the Prussian kings and emperors, of wars and the construction of the Wall, and of the Cold War and its consequences, which were more visible in this divided city than anywhere else in the world. History is never finished in Berlin. If you live here, you are part of it. Today, what the chronicler Walter Kiaulehn wrote in 1958 still holds true, "You don't have to be born a Berliner. You can become one."

The tallest circus tent in the world is on Potsdamer Platz. Designed by Helmut Jahn, the roof is suspended above the Sony Center forum.

The German capital is an independent state within the Federal Republic. Covering some 890 sq km (344 sq miles), Berlin is the country's largest and most populous city with 3.4 million inhabitants. Among its population, 447,000 are foreign, including 130,000 Turks and just over 32,000 Poles. The religious patchwork of the city is made up of roughly 867,000 Protestants, 31,000 Catholics, 20,3000 Muslims and 11,000 Jews.

CONTENTS

Below: view of the large cupola hall in the Bode Museum, which was reopened in 2006 on Berlin's Museum Island. In the middle stands an equestrian statue of Friedrich Wilhelm, the "Great Elector." The inset below depicts four generations: in the coach, Wilhelm I (1797–1888) and Friedrich Wilhelm (1882–1951), on horseback Friedrich III (1831–1888) and Wilhelm II (1859–1941).

TIMELINE

Berlin's history is short compared to other German cities, but it balances brevity with significance. Germany's largest metropolis is first mentioned in official documents in the 13th century. From then on, it developed at a breakneck pace. It has seen many rulers, including prince electors, Prussian kings and German emperors, and was often a center for art and culture. Today, the old and new capital has made a vibrant recovery from its darkest hours during the Nazi dictatorship and the subsequent Cold War division.

The Hohenzollern dynasty (right) began in 1415 and provided an unbroken line of prince electors and rulers who resided in Berlin. They included figures such as Friedrich II (1440–1470), Albrecht III Achilles (1470–1486), Johann Cicero (1486–1499), Joachim I Nestor (1499–1535), Joachim II Hector (1535–1571), Johann Georg (1571–1598), Joachim Friedrich (1598–1608) and Johann Sigismund (1608–1619). Hohenzollern rule came to an in 1918 with Wilhelm II, who had succeeded his father, Friedrich III, in 1888 and was both emperor of Germany and king of Prussia.

1232, 1237, 1244
Spandau, Cölln and Berlin are first mentioned in official documents.

1307
The twin towns of Berlin and Cölln merge to form a union.

July 1320
Heinrich II dies, the last margrave from the house of Ascania.

1348
The plague decimates the populations of Berlin and Cölln.

January 10, 1356
Emperor Karl IV grants the status of prince elector to the margrave of Brandenburg.

1359
After a union lasting for nearly fifty years, Berlin and Cölln join the Hanseatic League.

In 1417, Friedrich I von Hohenzollern is made elector of the march of Brandenburg.

Medieval twin cities

Present-day Berlin was born out of an amalgamation of towns and villages that had mostly been founded in the 13th century. The historic core was then formed by the towns Berlin and Cölln, which developed around the Nikolai district (Berlin) and the island (Cölln) on the other side of the Spree river. Cölln was first mentioned in official records in the year 1237, while Berlin appears just seven years later, in 1244. Archaeological excavations indicate that both towns had existed for some time by then and had developed from the settlements of German merchants and artisans. Berlin-Cölln enjoyed an exceptionally favorable location at the crossroads of the trading routes between Leipzig and Szczecin (form. Stettin) and Magdeburg and Wroclaw (form. Breslau). Furthermore, a shipping route joined the region with the major port city of Hamburg. Berlin and Cölln quickly developed into a flourishing trade city and transhipment point for long-distance commerce. In the 14th century, both towns joined the Hanseatic League, but they never attained the stature that Cologne, Hamburg or Antwerp enjoyed.

As early as 1307, Berlin and Cölln had merged to form a union. A magistrature consisting of twelve councillors from Berlin and six from Cölln now determined the fate of the town. A town wall was built around both Berlin and Cölln at the end of the 13th century. It was first referred to in records in

1319 and its remains can still be seen today near Klosterstrasse.

Disquieting times followed in the 14th century as the plague epidemic of 1348 killed off part of the population and large fires caused extensive damage in both 1376 and 1380. Added to this was political turmoil. In 1320, when the last margrave from the House of Ascania died, Heinrich II, Brandenburg was threatened with total chaos and anarchy. The territorial lords changed frequently at the time, and control of the Margraviate of Brandenburg was fiercely contested. Stability did not reign again until 1415, when Friedrich VI von Hohenzollern, then Burgrave of Nuremberg,

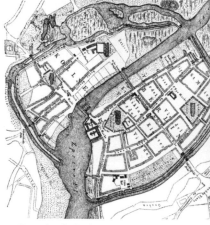

Berlin and Cölln in the year 1250.

was given the status of Margrave of Brandenburg. The mighty House of Hohenzollern would ultimately rule Brandenburg for nearly five hundred years.

1415
Friedrich I von Hohenzollern is made margrave of Brandenburg.

1451
Berlin-Cölln becomes the seat of the prince-elector.

1539
Prince-elector Joachim II von Brandenburg converts to Protestantism.

1631, 1635
Berlin-Cölln is besieged by Swedish troops.

November 8, 1685
With the Edict of Potsdam, Brandenburg grants religious freedom and sanctuary to the Huguenots.

Mai 9, 1688
Prince-Elector Friedrich Wilhelm I dies in Potsdam.

Berlin – seat of the elector

Under its new rulers, Berlin lost much of its municipal independence. In 1432, the elector divided the combined municipal administration of Berlin and Cölln and decreed that in future both towns had to form their own councils. The structure of the council, furthermore, had to be confirmed by the territorial lord. In 1442, Cölln was forced to cede a site on Werder Island in the Spree river for the prince-elector's new palace. Construction was completed by 1451, and Berlin-Cölln became the new electoral seat. The palace, however, was regarded with disdain by the citizens as it was not designed to defend against outside enemies but rather as a refuge to fend off potential local unrest. Accordingly, the edifice became locally known as "Zwing Cölln" (fortress Cölln).

Berlin and Cölln survived the Reformation in the first half of the 16th century quite peaceably and without bloodshed. As it turned out, many of the city's inhabitants actually preferred the new faith, including Prince-Elector Joachim II, who converted to Protestantism in 1539. Joachim's reign, which lasted more than three decades from 1535 to 1571, was characterized by feverish construction activity. In addition to the electoral palace, he had

a number of country mansions built: Köpenick to the east, Potsdam to the west, and the hunting lodge in Grunewald.

During the Thirty Years' War (1618–1648), hostile enemy troops marched repeatedly through Brandenburg, which had no army to speak of, and devastated the countryside. Although the towns of Berlin and Cölln escaped military conquest, they were besieged several times by Swedish troops who demanded exorbitant protection payments. In addition, Berlin and Cölln were stricken by plague epidemics five times during this period and the population dwindled by half from around 12,000 to just 6,000. The economic backbone of trade and industry was also largely destroyed by the outbreaks.

During the reign of young Friedrich Wilhelm I, reconstruction of the town after the war brought an economic upswing to Berlin-Cölln. The prince-elector even brought in settlers, mainly from Holland. The Edict of Potsdam from 1685 guaranteed their religious freedom, which then attracted a further 5,000 or so Huguenots who had been expelled from France. They settled mainly in Dorotheenstadt. Together with Friedrichswerder and Friedrichstadt, it was one of three baroque suburbs built during the nearly fifty-year reign of Friedrich Wilhelm I. When the "Great Elector" died in 1688, the number of inhabitants had once again reached 18,000, three times as many as at the beginning of his reign.

Friedrich Wilhelm von Hohenzollern, also known as the "Great Elector," ruled from 1640 to 1688.

Right: Friedrich I was the first king of Prussia and reigned from 1701 to 1713. He had succeeded his father, Friedrich Wilhelm, as elector of Brandenburg as early as 1688. His portrait was painted around 1701. Middle: In 1713, Friedrich's son was bequeathed with the title King Friedrich Wilhelm I, which he held until his death in 1740. Because he was responsible for Prussia's rise to military power, he was named the "Soldier King". The painting shows him in about 1733. Far right: After Friedrich I's death, Friedrich II "the Great" took over power and reigned until 1786. He was a great supporter of the arts and music.

January 18, 1701
Prince-Elector Friedrich III has himself crowned king of Prussia.

January 17, 1709
Berlin, Cölln and three suburbs band together as the "capital and royal residence Berlin."

February 25, 1713
Friedrich Wilhelm I becomes king of Prussia and begins building up the army.

1719
According to the first census, Berlin has 64,000 inhabitants.

May 31, 1740
The "Soldier King" dies and his son, Friedrich II, ascends the throne.

1740
The center of Berlin is given a facelift. The new grand plaza is called the "Forum Fridericianum". Today it is Bebelplatz.

James Kirkland, a grenadier in Friedrich Wilhelm I's "Giant Guards"

Soldier town and royal residence

The expansion of Berlin as the seat of Prussian nobility continued under Friedrich III, son and successor of the "Great Elector". Given the city's status as royal residence as of 1701, the elector was granted the right to be crowned king of Prussia by Emperor Leopold I. As a result, the king also wanted Berlin's new status as a capital of European importance – on a par with Paris and London, for example – to be evident in its grand architecture. The first of the baroque masterpieces here were constructed along the boulevard Unter den Linden and include the Zeughaus, which was completed in 1706 and served as a weapons arsenal.

Even before his (self) coronation, Friedrich III had his city palace remodelled by architect and sculptor Andreas Schlüter in order to bring it in line with the styles of the day. For his wife, Sophie Charlotte, the king commissioned a palace near the village of Lietzow to the west of the town. Initially known as Schloss Lietzenburg, both the palace and the villages around it were renamed Charlottenburg when Sophie died in 1705.

In the year 1709, the towns of Berlin, Cölln, Friedrichs-werder, Dorotheenstadt and Friedrichstadt were combined into a single town: the "capital and royal residence of Berlin." At that point in time, the city's population had already climbed to 55,000, and it was expanding rapidly. After the first census in 1719, some 64,000 people were living in Berlin and every fifth person was a Huguenot – religiously persecuted Protestants who had immigrated all the way from France after 1685.

When the "Soldier King" Friedrich Wilhelm I began his reign in 1713, life in Berlin took on a military character. The new ruler was less interested in representative buildings than in the development of the Prussian army. Many places in town became parade grounds such as today's Pariser Platz. Spurred on by the burgeoning army's growing need for new uniforms, Berlin became a natural center for the textiles industry. The "Royal Warehouse" on Klosterstrasse alone employed some 4,000 textile workers, making it Europe's largest fabric mill. In fact, the production of silk also contributed greatly to the economic rise of Berlin during this period. Although the military continued to define the city's outward appearance, the intellectual climate was transformed almost instantly when the "Soldier King" died in 1740. The new king, Friedrich II, wished to transform Berlin into a European center of the Enlightenment where culture and the sciences would flourish. A group of scholars, writers and educated citizens began flocking to Berlin publisher Friedrich Nicolai and Jewish philosopher Moses Mendelssohn, and meeting in "clubs" and "societies" to discuss and debate the philosophical, scientific and political questions of the day.

Immediately after ascending the throne, Friedrich II set about giving Berlin a new, more prestigious city center along the future boulevard Unter den Linden. It was to be called the "Forum Fridericianum" and would ultimately comprise the Opernhaus (opera), completed in 1743, the St Hedwigskirche, the Königliche Bibliothek (the royal library) and the Prinz-Heinrich-Palais, which is now Humboldt University.

When Friedrich II died in 1786, Berlin had about 150,000 inhabitants, and was one of the largest cities in Europe. However, the Prussian capital was still far from being considered a cosmopolitan metropolis. Beyond the relatively few grand boulevards in the center, visitors to Berlin did not encounter much glitz or glamour. In fact, historical documentation speaks of unkempt and unlit streets, of drastic housing shortages and rampant prostitution. Large sections of the lower classes, who had settled mainly in the northern and eastern suburbs, lived in dire poverty. At times of great need, for example in 1761, at the height of the Seven Years' War, as many as a third of Berlin's population had to rely on alms and municipal soup kitchens.

Berlin 1688–1786
Capital of the Prussian Kingdom

December 1740
Friedrich II invades Silesia with his troops.

1744–1745
During the Second Silesian War, Friedrich II's army defeats the Austrians.

1756–1763
The Seven Years' War against Austria, Russia and Saxony leads to economic crisis.

1757 and 1760
Austrian and Russian troops occupy Berlin.

1770
Unter den Linden is expanded and upgraded as a grand boulevard.

August 17, 1786
Friedrich II dies in Potsdam at the age of 74 after a forty-year reign.

This painting from 1763 shows Friedrich II the Great wearing the medal of the Order of the Black Eagle.

Friedrich II as commander

Friedrich II "the Great" is mainly known today as an Enlightenment figure and modernizer as well as an avid patron of the arts and sciences. However, his goal of securing a place for Prussia in the ranks of European cultural superpowers was tainted by three wars of aggression that Friedrich II carried out despite "controversial" interpretation of international law.

In December 1740, roughly six months after ascending the Prussian throne, Friedrich II and his Prussian army invaded Silesia, which at that time belonged to Austria. The First Silesian War began in the summer of 1742, and ended with the conquest of the territory. Prussia also won the Second Silesian War against Austria in 1744–1745. Later, during the so-called Seven Years' War (1756–1763), however, a coalition of Russia, Austria, France, Sweden and Saxony nearly defeated the Prussians on several occasions despite an alliance with Great Britain. Berlin itself was directly affected by this conflict: in 1757 and again in 1760, enemy forces occupied the city, departing only after extortionate tolls had been paid.

History, particularly during the 19th century, painted a flowery picture of Friedrich II as an ingenious commander-in-chief who, for a long time, enjoyed a reputation of invincibility. And this myth still lives on even today. Indeed, what is certain is that Friedrich II – unlike other rulers of

Friedrich II the Great with his regiment.

his time – personally participated and fought in all of his wars, leading his troops into battle alongside his generals. Evidently, he was wont to ignore the danger to his own life, preferring to fully immerse himself in the midst of combat – and not always to the delight of his fellow commanders. On several such occasions, the monarch's mount was shot dead as he rode, and on several others he only narrowly escaped death from hostile rounds.

At the turn of the 19th century, intellectual and scientific life in Berlin was shaped by numerous literary figures, philosophers, scholars and scientists who had come to the flourishing metropolis from far and wide. Among these personalities were (right): August Wilhelm von Schlegel (1767–1845), Friedrich von Schlegel (1772–1829), Wilhelm von Humboldt (1767–1835), Clemens Brentano (1778–1842), Heinrich von Kleist (1777–1811), Adelbert von Chamisso (1781–1838), Alexander von Humboldt (1769–1859) and brothers Jacob and Wilhelm Grimm (1785–1863, 1786–1859), authors of the legendary fairy tales.

August 17, 1786
Friedrich II's nephew, Friedrich Wilhelm II, becomes king of Prussia.

November 16, 1797
Friedrich Wilhelm II dies. His son, Friedrich Wilhelm III, succeeds him on the throne.

August 14, 1806
In the battle of Jena and Auerstedt, Prussia is defeated by the troops of Napoleon I.

1806–1808
French troops occupy Berlin.

October 9, 1807
In Brandenburg-Prussia, serfdom among the peasant population is abolished.

April 1809
For the first time, free and secret elections take place in Berlin for city parliament.

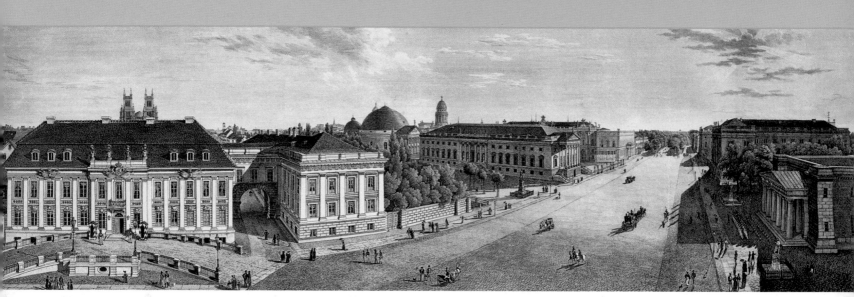

This copper etching by Carl Pescheck from the year 1830 shows the view of Unter den Linden boulevard from the Zeughaus.

Between reform and restoration

Since Friedrich II had no children of his own, he was succeeded in

Friedrich Wilhelm II (1744–1797)

Friedrich Wilhelm III (1770–1840)

1786 by his nephew, Friedrich Wilhelm II. Unlike his predecessor, the new king thought little of the ideas of the Enlightenment, preferring instead to increase censorship. Despite this, it seems nothing could keep Berlin at the turn of the 19th century from developing into a center for intellectual life: poets and thinkers such as Friedrich von Schlegel, Wilhelm and Alexander von Humboldt, Johann Gottlieb Fichte and Ludwig Tieck met frequently in the salons of mostly Jewish ladies to debate lyrically on the subjects of philosophy, art and literature. Many of these figures were apolitical, tending more towards the ideals of Romanticism.

After the devastating defeat of the Prussian army at Jena and Auerstedt, Napoleon and his troops marched into Berlin in the autumn of 1806. The two years of the occupation weighed heavily on Berliners, for the city, which now had about 170,000 inhabitants, was forced to pay the costs of billeting the French army. As a special humiliation, the Quadriga, a four-horse chariot crowning the Brandenburg Gate that had been completed in 1791, was taken to France by Napoleon.

After the departure of the French in 1809, the Prussian king and the royal household returned from Königsberg (today's Kaliningrad) where they had fled after the defeat to the French. Extensive reforms were introduced in order to bring the Prussian state in line with the demands of modern times. Serfdom had already been abolished in 1807. This was followed by extensive changes in the military, administration and education systems, and the renowned University of Berlin was founded in 1809. In the same year, Berliners were allowed for the first time to elect delegates to the municipal council.

In 1812, the French army again invaded Berlin, but it was finally defeated in the liberation wars of 1813 to 1815. Shortly thereafter, this brief period of reforms in Prussia ended, and the power of the monarchy was restored. In 1819, a wave of arrests in Berlin affected anyone with nationalist, liberal or democratic views, including the "Father of Gymnastics," Friedrich Ludwig Jahn, and heralded decades of suppression for what was a promising scene for liberals and intellectuals in Berlin.

November 2, 1809
Teaching starts at the University of Berlin.

December 23, 1809
King Friedrich Wilhelm III returns to Berlin from Königsberg (Kaliningrad).

1812
Napoleon's troops once again occupy Berlin.

1813
Napoleon I is defeated in the Battle of the Nations at Leipzig, and withdraws his army.

1818
Renowned architect Karl Friedrich Schinkel builds the Neue Wache on Unter den Linden.

July 14, 1819
In the course of the anti-liberal restoration, Friedrich Ludwig Jahn, the "father of gymnastics," is arrested.

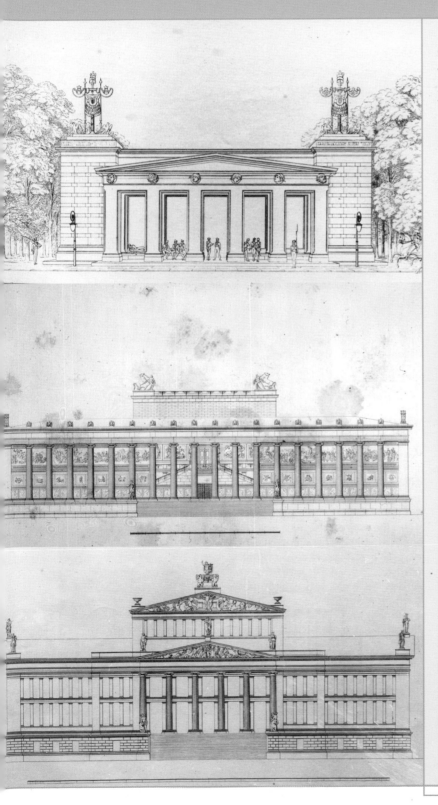

The architect of neoclassical Berlin

Architect, painter and theater set designer, Karl Friedrich Schinkel (1781–1841), left an unrivalled mark on Berlin's magnificent 19th-century cityscape. Schinkel was behind the construction of over fifty projects in the Prussian capital, including the Tegeler Schloss, the Friedrichswerdersche Kirche and the Bauakademie between the Schleusen and Schloss bridges.

Karl Friedrich Schinkel was born the son of a vicar in the small Brandenburg town of Neuruppin on March 13, 1781. After his father's untimely death, the family moved to Berlin in 1794, where he enrolled at the Graues Kloster (monastery) grammar school. The talented youth expressed an early enthusiasm for the arts, but ultimately decided to become an architect.

Schinkel's architectural ideals were influenced by the classics of antiquity, which he saw during a course in Italy in 1803 to 1805. After returning, Schinkel initially worked as a painter and set designer. In 1810, thanks to some help from Wilhelm von Humboldt, he was appointed senior assessor of construction. Only five years later, he was promoted to the position of "Oberbaurat," or chief government building surveyor. From his office on the Gendarmenmarkt, Schinkel was charged with giving Berlin, an unspectacular city at the time, a more elegant and prestigious look. His first major project in the capital was the Neue Wache on Unter den Linden. Completed in 1818, it established Schinkel's reputation as Landesbaumeister (state architect). A few years later, it was followed by the Schauspielhaus (theater), the Schlossbrücke (bridge) and the Altes Museum on Museum Island.

In 1830, Schinkel was appointed Oberbaudirektor (chief director of construction), and five years later as Oberlandesbaudirektor (chief state director of construction). Only a few years later, how-

Karl Friedrich Schinkel (1781–1841)

ever, in September 1840, he suffered a stroke and was paralyzed on one side. Karl Friedrich Schinkel died in Berlin on October 9, 1841, at the age of 60.

Left, from top: Neue Wache, Altes Museum on Museum Island and the Schauspielhaus on Gendarmenmarkt by Karl Friedrich Schinkel.

Right: The railway is regarded as synony-
mous with the industrialization of Europe.
In Germany, one of the earliest locomotives
was "the first Borsig locomotive" of 1841.
It was produced in the Berlin factory of
entrepreneur, August Borsig, for use on the
Berlin-Potsdam railway. Only three years
later, the Borsig plant built the slightly more

advanced "Beuth" model. It dif-
fered only in minor details from
the earlier model, but over the
next few decades, the railway
underwent major changes. This
is evident from the 1875 locomotive with coal tender, which ran
on the Berlin-Hamburg line.

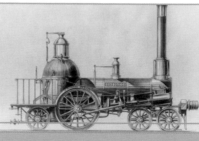

1825–1841	1838	1839	1840	1841	1848
The incorporation of several surrounding villages increases Berlin's area threefold, to 5,923 hectares (14,636 acres).	The opening of the line to Potsdam heralds the start of the railway age for Berlin.	For the first time, horse-drawn cabs operate in Berlin to speed up cross-town traffic.	Friedrich Wilhelm IV is crowned king of Prussia in Berlin.	August Borsig introduces his first locomotive to the public at Anhalter station.	Intellectuals and students lead citizens against the monarchy.

Revolution 1848–1849

Following the first riots in Vienna on March 11, 1848, hostilities quickly spread to the Prussian capital and by March 18, mass demonstrations led to the military opening fire on citizens who were forcefully voicing their demands. Naturally, the situation escalated, barricades were put up, and the people began arming themselves for continued conflict. After a bloody battle in which some 300 people were killed, Friedrich Wilhelm IV relented. He withdrew his troops from Berlin and agreed to, among other things, form a national assembly that was to write a constitution for Prussia. In the following months, however, the democratic forces among the revolutionaries were unable to maintain the upper hand. When rioting broke out between demonstrators and the citizen militia, the king quickly made use of the opportunity, sending in troops to restore order in the city. The spirit of the movement faltered and the revolution died.

From top: Rioting in 1848; barricade on Neue Königstrasse; King Friedrich Wilhelm IV out riding; 1849, the Frankfurt National Assembly invests the king with the rank of emperor of the Germans.

A city under pressure

Until the beginning of the 19th century, Berlin was first and foremost the seat of the Prussian king. It was also a military and manufacturing town with a popu-

as a capital also had a positive effect. Even industrial espionage was contributing to the city's rise. Among those involved in this was Berlin entrepreneur and calico printing factory

Industrialization transforms the cityscape: Borsig's engineering works (1847).

lation of just over 170,000. But the technological innovations arriving from England in the 18th century – among them the steam engine, the "spinning jenny", and the railway – were awakening Berlin from its slumber. Important impulses here also came from the changes in the basic economic and political conditions in Germany. In 1810, for example, free trade was introduced. In 1834, customs barriers were removed, creating a large, unified market. And finally, in the 1840s, the construction of the first railway tracks revolutionized the country's traffic and transportation networks. Berlin's long tradition as a commercial center and its inflated importance

King Friedrich Wilhelm IV in 1850

Berlin 1838–1871
Berlin as a center of industry

1850
First election of delegates to the municipal council with the new three-class voting rights.

1860–1869
Construction of the new city hall in the Mitte district, based on plans by Karl Friedrich Schinkel.

1861
The incorporation of outlying villages enlarges the urban area by 70 per cent.

1862
The "plan for the development of greater Berlin" determines the layout of roads in the new outlying areas.

1869
From now on, Berlin's sewage is channelled to sewage farms outside the city.

1871
After the proclamation of the king as Emperor Wilhelm I, Berlin is elevated to the status of capital of the empire.

owner, Johann Friedrich Dannenberger. As a result of all this, the 1830s marked the beginning of the city's transformation into an industrial power. Increasing numbers of people moved

population had more than doubled, to just under 400,000. By 1871, when the German Empire was founded, it had increased by a further 370,000. With the population boom came increased demand for accommodation. Cur-

the case of a fire, hoses could be maneuvered and rescue nets opened. The living conditions inside the tiny, poorly lit one- or two-bedroom apartments were imaginably bad while oc-

Zille's milieu

No one has been able to document the social conditions in Berlin's working-class districts as accurately as Heinrich Zille (1858–1929), a local graphic

Adolph von Menzel's *Steel Rolling Mill* (1875) shows the dire working conditions.

August Borsig, Werner von Siemens

Backyard with painting by Zille.

to Berlin not only from the outlying areas but from other countries in search of jobs. In addition to textiles, the engineering and metal industries had developed into leading sectors by the 1870s. At the beginning of the century, only one engineering company had existed in Berlin. Over the next sixty years, 67 companies had been established, employing well over 5,000 workers.

Berlin's boom had massive effects on the city, in terms of both geography and social composition. By the middle of the century, the

rent space was insufficient and the housing shortage escalated.
Around the old heart of the city, beyond the 18th-century customs walls, the so-called Wilhelminian belt of tenement blocks sprang up. Housing blocks four to six floors high dominated this densely built-up area. The complexes had multiple wings that were only accessible via an inner courtyards. Property developers were basically given a blank check when building these tenements. According to a municipal building inspection decree of 1853, builders only had to ensure that the inner courtyards covered a minimum surface area of no less than 5.34 x 5.34 m (5.83 x 5.83 yds), so that in

cupancy was very high. In 1869, the mortality rate in these working-class districts was twice as high as that in middle-class areas.
Populations were growing rapidly in the villages surrounding Berlin as well. In 1871, Charlottenburg and Spandau, for example, already had populations of 19,587 and 20,451, respectively. The future Neukölln had 8,125 residents, and Köpenick in the east had 5,265. Farm settlements like Pankow and Lichtenberg had grown to more than 3,000 inhabitants in just a matter of years.

artist, illustrator and photographer. He observed everyday life and the living conditions of workers and middle-class citizens in the streets and in the crammed rear wings of the tenement blocks. Zille put what he saw onto paper and peppered it with irony and wit. His work reveals a critical view of the social conditions during the industrialization of Berlin.

To the right: On January 18, 1871, in the Hall of Mirrors at the palace of Versailles, King Wilhelm I of Prussia is officially declared German emperor. This painting of the proclamation dates from 1885. Having been king of Prussia since 1861, Wilhelm I became emperor one decade later. This portrait shows him in 1870. In 1888, Wilhelm I's son, Friedrich III, ruled as king of Prussia, and as Emperor Friedrich I, for only ninety-nine days. His son, Wilhelm II, succeeded him to the throne in the same year, 1888, and ruled until 1918, when he abdicated and went into exile in the Netherlands. He died there in 1941.

The monarch and the imperial chancellor: Wilhelm I receives Bismarck in the historic corner room of the royal palace.

Berlin – imperial capital

In 1871, Prussian King Wilhelm I was proclaimed German emperor and the former prime minister, Count Otto von Bismarck, became the chancellor. As a result, Berlin, the largest city in Germany, became the capital of the new empire, further accelerating the already dynamic growth of the city. Berlin's population virtually exploded on the news: in 1877, the city had more than one million people and less than thirty years later that number exceeded two million. The subsequent housing shortage was predictably drastic, especially since continued

A color postcard from 1905, showing the "Unter den Linden" boulevard.

A view of Friedrichstrasse with the station of the same name (1915).

Berlin 1871–1918
Berlin in the time of the emperors

1905
Berlin's population exceeds two million for the first time.

Spring 1907
The Kaufhaus des Westens (KaDeWe) opens on Wittenbergplatz.

1913
In Berlin, construction of the AVUS begins, the first motorway in the world.

August 1914
World War I breaks out, to the jubilation of Berlin. War fever is upon them.

After 1917
Strikes and mass demonstrations against war and famine take place in Berlin.

November 9, 1918
Wilhelm II abdicates as German emperor and goes into exile in the Netherlands.

development within the city soon reached maximum capacity. Construction activities were thus focused on outlying settlements: today's district of Schöneburg rose during the same period from 20,000 to more than 300,000. Aside from the old inner city around Friedrichstrasse, a second center developed around Kurfürstendamm, with classy shopping

The Reichstag was built between 1884 and 1894. This photograph is from 1898.

After its completion in 1905, the Berliner Dom dominates its surroundings.

berg, for example, which in 1871 had only 4,500 people, had grown into a large city of more than 200,000 by 1910. The population of the "boom town" Charlotten-

malls and large department stores. The most famous of these was the Kaufhaus des Westens (the KaDeWe, "department store in the west") on Wittenbergplatz. It opened in 1907 and was still

considered the largest of its kind on the continent a century later.

By 1890, all homes in Berlin had been connected to the public water supply, and construction of a municipal sewer system led to great improvements in hygiene for the city. The public transport system was also taking shape. In 1902, Berlin's first subway was put into operation, running overground on today's U1 and U2 underground lines between the Warschauer Brücke and Zoologischer Garten. One of the other important projects of the day was the world's first motorway, the AVUS (automobile traffic and exercise street), built between 1913 and 1921 in Berlin.

This new era of rapid development also left its mark in architectural terms. By the turn of the 20th century, Schinkel's neoclassical style had been replaced by Historicism and "Wilhelminian Baroque," as seen in the Berliner Dom (cathedral). This relatively pompous style got its name from the aesthetic preferences of Emperor Wilhelm II (1888–1918), who also had a profound political effect on the city and the empire. Adhering to the typically aggressive politics of a superpower, he was determined to assert a dominant position in Europe for the Germans. Only a few years later he happily led the country into World War I.

World War I

Berlin, August 1914: Like many other German cities, the population is gripped by war fever. Even in the rear wings of poor working-class tenement blocks, flags hang out of the windows each time a victory is reported. As the war drags on, and in the

From top: Parade, 1914; Paul von Hindenburg, Wilhelm II and Erich Ludendorff; troops coming home in 1918.

face of increasingly strained supply lines, however, enthusiasm for the cause soon wanes and eventually the city, and the country, turns on its leaders. Starting in 1917, mass demonstrations and strikes become the order of the day. After the German empire is defeated, the unrest culminates in the November Revolution of 1918.

The first two decades of the 20th century afforded little room for artistic or cultural endeavors. Between World War I and World War II, however, the cultural scene in Berlin and Europe flourished. Despite many artists and poets being persecuted or emigrating during the Nazi period, many managed to retain their place in German cultural history.

Among them were signifcant figures such as (right): Bertolt Brecht (1898–1956), Alfred Döblin (1878–1957), Heinrich Mann (1871–1950), Carl von Ossietzky (1889–1938), Kurt Tucholsky (1890–1935), Franz Werfel (1890–1945) and Stefan Zweig (1881–1942).

November 9, 1918
Max von Baden announces the emperor's abdication, against the latter's will.

November 9, 1918
Philipp Scheidemann and Karl Liebknecht both declare the establishment of separate republics for Germany.

December 1918
The "Stahlhelm" (steel helmet) Spartacus League and the left-wing radical KPD (Communist Party of Germany) are founded.

January 15, 1919
The Spartacus uprising is put down by the government; Rosa Luxemburg and Karl Liebknecht are murdered by the right-wing Freikorps militia.

March 1919
The military puts down a general strike, 1,200 people die.

March 13, 1920
Wolfgang Kapp declares himself Chancellor; the Kapp Putsch is defeated after only a few days.

1918–1919: revolution, rebellion and strike

Internal political struggle began in earnest in Germany after the November Revolution of 1918. On November 9, 1918, the day that the Chancellor, Max von Baden, announced the emperor's abdication, two men in Berlin declared the establishment of the republic: Socialist Philipp Scheidemann and Communist Karl Liebknecht.

From top: a machine gun in position; defense on top of the Brandenburg Gate; exchanging fire on Bülowplatz.

Fierce controversy over the future of the nation ensued, initially in the form of debate and later in the form of uprisings (January and March of 1919). Both were put down by bloody government reprisals.

Center for the arts and glamour

Once the political situation in Germany had stabilized after 1923, the economy also continued to recover from the effects of World

Famous actors, from left: Hans Albers, Emil Jannings, Gustaf Gründgens and Fritz Kortner.

Famous actresses, from left: Tilla Durieux as Salome, Marlene Dietrich, Fritzi Massary and Greta Garbo.

War I. As prosperity among the population slowly rose, influenced by the rapid development of radio and cinema, people shrugged off the traumas of the preceding ten years. Berlin became a city of the avant-garde and Expressionists, of cinema and theater, and of comedy and cabaret. With the construction of the huge Capitol and Ufa-Palast movie houses, Kurfürstendamm became the meeting point of choice for young filmgoers. At the new venues that sprang up like mushrooms throughout the city, jazz music and the Charleston fired up dancers and revellers. Famous musicians celebrated their triumphs in Berlin, including Duke Ellington, who stayed here with his "Chocolate Kiddies" in 1924, and Josephine Baker, who was the talk of the town in 1927, especially thanks to her flimsy outfit. Revues and variety shows also offered entertainment to the tireless patrons. Singers and comedians such as Claire Waldoff and Otto Reutter were thus able to excite audiences in places like the legendary Berlin Wintergarten throughout the 1920s. When imperial censorship of theater was abolished at the end of World War I, cabarets and small venues

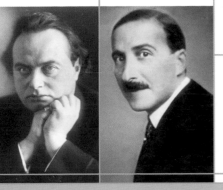

Berlin 1919–1929
The "Golden Twenties"

July 15, 1920
Eight towns and fifty-nine communes are incorporated to create Greater Berlin.

1922
Marc Chagall moves to Berlin. Wilhelm Furtwängler conducts the Philharmonic Orchestra.

June 1923
Hyperinflation reigns. Four million people live in Berlin; 235,000 are unemployed.

1924
Berlin's first central airport is opened in Tempelhof.

1924 and 1926
In 1924, the First Radio Exhibition takes place; in 1926, the Funkturm (radio tower) is built.

1927
Heinrich Zille publishes *Bilder vom alten und neuen Berlin* (*Pictures of the Old and New Berlin*)

flourished around the city. Word of the liberal and open attitude travelled quickly, and the sophistication of the big city began attracting artists from around the world to Berlin. The avant-garde enjoyed a large audience, and the work of Expressionists, Surrealists and Dadaists were features in museums and galleries. The politics and culture of the day were reflected in the works of people like Carl Zuckmayer and Bertolt Brecht, whose plays *The Captain of Köpenick* and *The Threepenny Opera* premiered in Berlin before making their way around the world.

But the Roaring Twenties in Berlin came to an abrupt end in 1929, as the New York Stock Exchange plummeted on October 24. After "Black Thursday," the global economy experienced its most serious crisis since the end of the war. Mass unemployment and poverty struck the entire country, and the glitzy and glamorous metropolis was similarly affected.

In his novel, *Berlin Alexanderplatz*, Alfred Döblin portrays everyday life in the capital, noting that, in addition to the voices that were critical of society at the time, revanchist sounds could increasingly be heard in Berlin in the early 1930s. Indeed, the National Socialist takeover of the city in 1933 ushered in the end of Berlin's multicultural fabric.

Film metropolis Berlin

Berlin's reputation as a cinema city dates back to 1911, when the world's first large-scale film studio was opened nearby, in Babelsberg. Through the 1920s, Berlin managed to even increase its leading position in the industry, especially over its rival, Munich. In the first years after World War I, historical costume dramas such as *Fridericus Rex* (1922) enthralled moviegoers. Expressionist masterpieces like *The Cabinet of Dr Caligari* (1920),

The Blue Angel was filmed in 1930 (left); *Metropolis* in 1926 (above).

Dr Mabuse (1922) and *Nosferatu* (1922), received worldwide acclaim. Among Babelsberg Studios' most famous films was *Metropolis* (1926). It was even included in the UNESCO Memory of the World International Register in 2001. One of the most important directors of the silent film era was Fritz Lang, who emigrated to the United States in 1933.

Right: After defeat in World War II and the failure of the dictatorship, many important National Socialist figures committed suicide: Adolf Hitler shot himself on April 30, 1945, in his Berlin bunker; on October 15, 1946, just before his execution, Hermann Göring, commander of the German Luftwaffe, swallowed a capsule containing cyanide; Joseph Goebbels, who led the Reich Ministry for Popular Enlightenment and Propaganda, also took cyanide on May 1, 1945; the Reichsführer of the SS, Heinrich Himmler, killed himself on May 23, 1945, by swallowing a potassium cyanide capsule.

January 30, 1933
President Paul von Hindenburg appoints Adolf Hitler as Chancellor.

February 27-28, 1933
The Reichstag building catches fire and the Communists are charged with arson.

1934
Gustaf Gründgens becomes the new art director of the Staatliches Schauspielhaus, the state theater.

August 1, 1936
Opening ceremony of the Olympic Games. Leni Riefenstahl films the events.

1937
Berlin celebrates 700 years. Cölln was first mentioned in official records in 1237.

November 9-10, 1938
During the Reichskristallnacht, Jewish synagogues and businesses are vandalized.

Adolf Hitler speaks to followers on May 9, 1938, at the Berlin Lustgarten.

The end of culture

As the capital of the "Thousand-Year Reich," the fate of Berlin was inextricably linked with the political events of the 1930s and the grand plans of Adolf Hitler and his cohorts. The torchlight procession of the SA (Sturmabteilung, storm division) through the Brandenburg Gate on the day of Hitler's appointment as Chancellor of the Reich, as well as the Reichstag fire and the book burning on Opernplatz, when 20,000 books of an "un-Germanic spirit" were destroyed, are representative of the types of events that were taking place. Together they illustrate the political and social pressures that were exerted on the populace by the National Socialists. During the Olympic Games, which were held in Berlin in August 1936, the city served as a giant propaganda stage. The timing of the international sporting event perfectly suited the rulers of the day by helping them to divert the world's attention away from the criminal plans and radical events that were already taking place within the Reich.

The National Socialists had organized a complete restoration and reconstruction of Berlin. The city was to be transformed into the new capital and world metropolis of Germania. In 1937, Hitler appointed his star architect, Albert Speer, to the position of "Inspector general of construction in the capital of the Reich." Just one year later, Speer presented his overall concept for the project as well as some of the first detailed plans. Grand edifices and a giant cross with axes running in all directions of the compass constituted the core elements of his design. The focal point of the north-south axis was to be a grand boulevard 7 km (4.5 mi) in length and 156 m (171 yds) in width for military rallies and parades. Other monumental features of Speer's plan included construction of a gigantic "People's Hall" on Königsplatz and the Südbahnhof, which would be the largest station in the world. Speer began putting his plans into action in 1939, starting with the demolition of a handful of buildings on Tiergartenstrasse and some of the monuments on Königsplatz before broadening the east-west axis in the area where today the Avenue of June 17th runs. Berlin owes the lasting transformation of its cityscape, however, not just to National Socialist megalomania but also to its fate: Allied bombing basically reduced the city to ash and cinders. During the last few weeks of the war, in the so-called "Battle of Berlin," the Wehrmacht (German army), the Volkssturm (irregular army) and the Hitler Youth fought hopelessly in a house-to-house battle against the Red Army. By the time of capitulation, a third of the residential buildings had been destroyed and the population had fallen to 2.8 million.

Berlin 1933–1945
Berlin during the Nazi dictatorship

March 20, 1939
The Nazis burn "degenerate" art and empty the inventory of the Nationalgalerie.

October 18, 1941
Mass deportation of Berlin Jews to concentration and extermination camps begins.

January 20, 1942
At the Wannsee Conference, a final solution to "the Jewish question" is discussed.

February 18, 1942
In the Sportpalast, Joseph Goebbels incites the crowds to "total war."

April 30, 1945
Adolf Hitler commits suicide in the Führer's bunker in the Reichskanzlei (chancellery).

May 2, 1945
Capitulation after weeks of battles; the Soviet flag is raised over the Reichstag.

The dream of the One-Thousand-Year Empire

Adolf Hitler's appointment as Chancellor of the Reich and the last parliamentary elections, held in March of 1933, marked the beginning of Germany's darkest historical hour. With the aid of the Enabling Act of 1933, Hitler's new government first of all suspended the democratic constitution in order to then bring all of the organs of public life and justice under the control of the SS, SA and the Gestapo. Ideology and conduct were dictated by the image of the "pure Aryan" as the ideal human being, and the glorification of the peasantry, which was expressed in the ideology of "blood and soil." It was an imperative to ensure the survival of the "German people" and to protect it from hostile enemies. The National Socialists saw as their greatest enemies the "Bolshevist traitors of the fatherland," intellectuals and especially Jews, against whom they expressed their most egregious discrimination. The persecution of Jews reached fever pitch during the pogroms of the so-called Reichskristallnacht and the subsequent internment and execution in the infamous concentration and extermination camps.

Left, from top: Berlin in ruins; the Reichstag; May 2, 1945, soldiers hoist the Soviet flag from the destroyed Reichstag.

The invasion of Poland on September 1, 1939, was what finally triggered World War II. After initial successes, the tide turned in favour of the Allies starting in

Models of the new Berlin with (from top) Grosser Stern, Kongresshalle, and plaza.

1941. The NSDAP's dream of the Thousand-Year Reich ended in capitulation on May 8, 1945.

Because of West Berlin's unique political and geographical situation – "Berlin island" as it were – the city's mayors were always given special attention from the former Republic of Germany. After holding this esteemed office, some continued their careers on a federal level, including (at right): Ernst Reuter (1948–1953), whose name adorns one of the city's squares; Willy Brandt (1957–1966), who went on to become German chancellor from 1969 to 1974; Heinrich Albertz (1966–1967), who stepped down after the student riots; and Richard von Weizsäcker (1981–1984), German president for two terms.

1945
Berlin is placed under Allied control and divided into four sectors.

1947
During the winter of 1946, several hundred Berliners die of starvation and hypothermia.

1948
The German Mark is introduced in West Berlin.

June 24, 1948
Because of the Soviet blockade, western Allies spend nearly a year supplying the city in the Berlin Airlift.

January 11, 1955
Future Chancellor Willy Brandt (SPD) becomes the governing mayor of Berlin.

June 2, 1963
American President John F. Kennedy holds the famous "Ich bin ein Berliner" (I am a Berliner) speech.

The Berlin Airlift

On June 23, 1948, the military government of the western sectors of Berlin announced the introduction of the German Mark for the western half of the city. One day later, the Soviet military blocked all routes to Berlin. In response, the western Allies put together an "airlift": 380 planes, given the name "raisin bombers" by Berliners, operated around the clock to supply Berlin with all of the goods necessary to survive. During the blockade, which went on for nearly a year, supply planes flew into the city at 90-second intervals provid-

A "raisin bomber" making an approach in West Berlin during the Berlin Airlift.

ing a total of almost 1.8 million tons of goods in over 200,000 sorties. In order to relieve the Tempelhof Airport, a second airport was built at Tegel in the autumn of 1948. It was completed in just 62 days.

Window to the West

In 1945, at the end of World War II, Berlin was in ruins. For several years, the supply situation remained extreme-

Architectural icons of West Berlin (clockwise from top): Philharmonie, Gedächtniskirche; Kongresszentrum ICC; Kongresshalle.

ly tense, particularly since thousands of refugees from the former German areas in the east were flooding into the former German capital. On an administrative level, Berlin was divided into four sectors and placed under the sovereignty of the four wartime Allies. However, the increasingly pronounced differences between the three western powers and the Soviet Union quickly led to a gulf between East and West. West Berlin came to

represent the free world, and had to be protected from the grasp of the Soviet Union at all costs. During the Berlin blockade in 1948 and 1949, mayor Ernst Reuter launched a famous dramatic appeal to the international community for assistance to be provided to the trapped city: "People of the world, look upon this city!"

In the face of the wholesale exodus of businesses, West Berlin was not capable of sustaining itself economically and became unviable as a city. For decades, it was supported by massive subsidies, companies received tax concessions and employees were granted a so-called Berlin allowance. The area around Kurfürstendamm developed into a new center and

the Kulturforum was built close to the Wall along with the Philharmonie, the Neue Nationalgalerie museum and the Staatsbibliothek (State Library).

In the late 1960s, West Berlin began recruiting so-called "guest workers," mainly from Turkey, who now define neighborhoods like Kreuzberg, Neukölln and Wedding. West Berlin also attracted artists, conscientious objectors and students, and it was here that the civil rights and squatter movements of the 1960s gained momentum. Berlin has managed to retain its status as a center of alternative lifestyles to this day.

October 15, 1963
The Philharmonie in the Kultur-forum is inaugurated.

December 1, 1966
Governing Mayor Willy Brandt becomes foreign minister and moves to Bonn.

June 2, 1967
During a demonstration, student Benno Ohnesorg is shot down by the police.

April 11, 1968
Student leader. Rudi Dutschke, is seriously injured during an assassination attempt.

May 22, 1981
Squatter Klaus-Jürgen Rattay is fatally wounded during a demonstration.

November 9, 1989
Thousands of Berliners celebrate the fall of the Wall in the city center.

Atrium of the Willy Brandt House: a bronze statue of the politician, measuring 3.40 m (11 ft) tall and weighing 500 kg (1,102 lbs).

Willy Brandt

Apart from Richard von Weizsäcker, Willy Brandt, former chairman of the Social Democratic Party (SPD) and German chancellor, is one of the most important politicians to emerge from Berlin in the postwar era. In addition to those posts, Brandt was also mayor of West Berlin from 1957 to 1966.

Willy Brandt was born Herbert Frahm in Lübeck on Dezember 18, 1913, son of the unwed sales assistant Martha Frahm. Brandt, who was admitted to a top secondary school thanks to special aptitudes, was involved from an early age with the Socialist Workers' Youth. After the National Socialists took over, however, he emigrated to Norway where he worked as a journalist and ultimately assumed the name with which he would become famous: Willy Brandt.

In 1945, after the end of World War II, Willy Brandt was sent to Berlin as a correspondent for a number of Scandinavian newspapers. In 1949 he became a member of the German parliament for the SPD, and in 1950 was also elected to the Berlin senate. He was elected mayor in 1957 and succeeded Otto Suhr in that position. His resolute and unswirving demeanor following the 1958 Khrushchev ultimatum and the erection of the Berlin Wall made Willy Brandt exceptionally popular with Berliners.

Chairman of the SPD from 1964, Brandt moved to Bonn as foreign minister in 1966 before becoming German chancellor in 1969. The defining concept of his term was what he called *Ostpolitik*, a new way of dealing with the Soviet block that aimed at improving relations particularly with East Germany. At the time, Brandt faced serious criticism for the policy, but ultimately won the Nobel Peace Prize in 1971. In 1974, however, one of his closest colleagues, Günter Guillaume, was revealed as an East Germany spy

Willy Brandt and John F. Kennedy, Berlin

and Brandt was forced to resign. Having never come to terms with the division of Germany, it was he who, immediately after the fall of the Berlin Wall in 1989, coined the phrase: "What belongs together will now grow together." Willy Brandt only survived the reunification by a few years. He died on October 8, 1992, in Bonn.

The politburo of the Central Committee was the most important body of the East German socialist state and thus the political core of the GDR. Right: During a politburo meeting on July 26, 1968, Walter Ulbricht and Erich Honecker sit at the head of the table. Walter Ulbricht (1893–1973) had been the general secretary of the Central Committee since 1950 and chairman of the State Council since 1960. In 1971, Ulbricht was forced to resign his office. Erich Honecker (1912–1994) succeeded him during the final years of the GDR, finally resigning in 1989 and going into exile in Chile in 1993, where he died the following year.

The city of "real socialism"

When Berlin was divided into sectors, the occupying forces of the Soviet Union were given control of the districts Mitte, Prenzlauer Berg, Pankow, Friedrichshain, Treptow, Köpenick, Weissensee and Lichtenberg. As of 1949, they made up East Berlin, the capital of the GDR.

Compared with the western sectors, the eastern parts recovered only slowly economically, partly because the Soviet Union did not permit the Soviet zone of occupation to participate in the Marshall Plan for the reconstruction of Europe. In order to make the country more prosperous, however, the government of the GDR under Walter Ulbricht announced higher work quotas in 1952. But the range of available goods continued to decline, leading to a workers' uprising in 1953 that was suppressed by Soviet tanks on June 17.

In 1950, the GDR regime released its "Sixteen Principles of Socialist Urban Design", part of which would see East Berlin given a central axis that ran from the Brandenburg Gate via Alexanderplatz to Stalinallee (today's Frankfurter Allee). Since the end of the 1950s, Plattenbau (precast concrete slab) apartment blocks

Monument to Karl Marx and Friedrich Engels on Alexanderplatz.

had been sprouting up in the city center, and in the 1970s, massive residential developments such as Marzahn, Hohenschönhausen and Hellersdorf were built. The TV tower in the middle of Alexanderplatz was built in 1969, measuring 365 m (1,198 ft) and making it

From top: Palast der Republik, 1999; interior in 1985; demolition in 2006.

Europe's second-tallest building. In 1976, the Palast der Republik (palace of the republic) was built where once the Berlin city palace had stood. The GDR Volkskammer (people's parliament) had its seat here as well, and it was also a venue for cultural events. Because of its many lights, it was often lampooned as "Erichs Lampenladen" (Erich [Honecker's] lighting

shop). The GDR underwent a period of consolidation during the 1960s and 1970s, but in the mid-1980s, East Berlin and Leipzig became hotbeds of opposition to the Communist regime. The movement's activities, combined with a mass exodus over the Austria-Hungary border during the summer of 1989, led to the opening of the Berlin Wall on November 9, 1989, and ultimately to the dissolution of the GDR. As a legacy, many institutions in Berlin now exist in duplicate, for example the opera houses.

East Berlin 1945–1990
Capital of the GDR

Peter Fechter is one of the best-known victims of the Wall. On August 17, 1962, he was shot and left to bleed to death.

The Berlin Wall

Roughly three million people left the GDR between 1949 and 1961, most of them young, well educated and hoping for a better life in the West. When this mass exodus of emigrés began threatening the country's economy, units of the GDR's Nationale Volksarmee (national people's army) and the Volkspolizei (police) began barricading the border between the eastern and western sectors of Berlin in the early morning hours of August 13, 1961.

A concrete wall stretching 155 km (96 miles) and nearly 4 m (13 ft) high was built to enclose West Berlin and prevent any future escapes. If anyone tried to escape across the Wall, they often paid with their lives. On August 24, 1961, the shoot-to-kill order was put into action for the first time – with deadly consequences. The last victim of the order was twenty-year-old Chris Gueffroy in February 1989. It is still unclear exactly how many people were killed at the Wall between 1961 and 1989, but estimates vary between 80 and 230.

Soon after the opening of the German-Czech border, the GDR, in its final throes as a nation, began tearing down the Wall. Only a few sections remain today and have been placed under historic preservation orders, for example in Bernauer Strasse in the district Mitte. At important locations where the Wall has been removed, a line is set into the ground to

The Wall was still provisional in 1961.

commemorate its earlier course. This is particularly noticeable in the shadow of the modern buildings on Potsdamer Platz.

Germany's reunification and the decision to make Berlin the new capital provided the city with a unique opportunity to build a new government district. The core of this neighborhood now consists of the renovated Reichstag, which was rebuilt by internationally renowned architect Lord Norman Foster; the Bundeskanzleramt (federal chancellery) nearby, created by Axel Schultes and Charlotte Frank. Right: the glass dome of the Reichstag with the iconic Brandenburg Gate in the foreground; the illuminated Reichstag; a Bundestag (parliament) session in the Reichstag; Bundeskanzleramt.

October 2/3, 1990	June 20, 1991	1991	January 1, 1992	1993	May 5, 1996
Celebrations take place in Berlin to mark the first Day of German Unity.	The Bundestag moves parliamentary and government offices to Berlin.	The Rotes Rathaus on Alexanderplatz becomes the seat of Berlin's mayor.	Public transportation companies BVG (west) and BVB (east) are merged.	The President of the Republic transfers his seat to Berlin.	In a public referendum, the majority votes against fusing Berlin and Brandenburg.

After the fall of the Wall, from top: soldiers on top of the Wall; a curious soldier looking through a hole; celebrations and fireworks at the Brandenburg Gate; remains of the Wall near the Reichstag.

Reunification

After the fall of the Berlin Wall on November 9, 1989, demands for the reunification of the two German states were soon heard in both the East and West. Later that month, on November 28, 1989, Chancellor Helmut Kohl presented a ten-point program to the Bundestag that aimed at forming a confederation. Immediately after the elections to the GDR's parliament) on March 18, 1990, the federal government began negotiations with the GDR's leadership regarding an economic, monetary and social union. On July 1, it went into effect.

Once the victors from World War II had also come to an agreement in their "Two plus Four Talks", the path for German unity was cleared. On August 31, 1990, both Germanies signed the Unification Treaty and on October 3, 1990, hundreds of thousands of people in Berlin and other cities around the country celebrated the Day of German Unity, now a national holiday.

Berlin the capital

The reunification treaty between the GDR and the Federal Republic stated that Berlin should be the capital of the reunited Germany. However, it was controversial whether the city should also become the new seat of the government. Advocates for the two cities, Berlin and Bonn, were roughly divided across party lines. Eventually, on June 20, 1991, after a very heated and exceptionally emotional debate, a small parliamentary majority (338–320 votes) opted for a transfer of the seat of government to the city on the Spree, Berlin. In September 1999, the Deutscher Bundestag (parliament) began operating out of Berlin and one year later the Bundesrat (upper house) also transferred its seat to the Preussisches Herrenhaus in Leipziger Strasse near Potsdamer Platz.

Berlin politicians were also forced to move as a result of reunification. In 1991, the mayor's offices were moved from the Schöneberg town hall into the Rotes Rathaus on Alexanderplatz and the Senate was moved into the former Preussischer Landtag (Prussian parliament) in Stresemannstrasse.

During the euphoric first few years after reunification, many experts predicted a gigantic economic boom for the new capital. Unfortunately, little can be seen of such a positive development: neither the economy of West Berlin, which was heavily subsidized before 1990, nor the planned economy of East Berlin was able to make a smooth transition to a free market economy. Almost half of all jobs in industry in Berlin were lost in the 1990s. Today it is essentially the service sector that drives the city's economy. Tourism also developed particularly well. With continuously rising numbers, a record seven million foreign guests visited the city in 2006. Indeed, Berlin has established itself as an urban destination in Europe on a par with the cosmopolitan cities of Paris and London. In recent years, Berlin has also become increasingly important as a center for the sciences and media.

Unemployment rates still hover at 16 percent, much higher than the national average, and social problems have also become increasingly pronounced in districts such as Wedding, Neukölln and Kreuzberg, where a large percentage of the population is from abroad. Sadly, opportunities for politicians to implement countermeasures are limited by mounting debts of more than 63.5 billion euros (in 2006). Back in 2002, the Berlin Senate had already acknowledged that it was experiencing a budgetary state of emergency and sued for relief from the Federal Republic and other German states. The city's claim was sadly rejected by the Federal Constitutional Court in October 2006. Nevertheless, with a prolific music, theater and arts scene, the reunited Berlin has become a huge draw for young creative people from all over Europe.

Berlin 1990 to today
Capital of the Federal Republic of Germany

Under the cupola of the Sony Center on Potsdamer Platz, visitors enjoy the fountain, restaurants and eight cinemas.

Building site Berlin

Reunification also brought some massive changes for Berlin's skyline. Suddenly, construction was underway in every district. During the 1990s, Berlin was basically Europe's largest building site. In particular, the areas between the Reichstag, Potsdamer Platz and the Lehrter Stadtbahnhof (train station), which had been derelict until 1990, received a complete facelift.

Following designs from Renzo Piano, Christoph Kohlbecker and other famous architects, a shiny new city center was constructed on Potsdamer Platz between 1991 and 2000. The Sony Center, a steel and glass construction designed by Helmut Jahn, is one of the featured attractions. It consists of seven individual buildings around a domed central forum.

From 2003 to 2005, a huge field of columns was built between Potsdamer Platz and Brandenburg Gate: the "Memorial to the Murdered Jews of Europe", designed by architect Peter Eisenman from the United States. The transfer of parliamentary and governmental offices from Bonn to Berlin also generated a significant amount of construction as well. The new government district was established near the Reichstag and features office blocks, the Chancellery and a housing complex in a bend on the Spree that was originally in-

From top: Academy of Art; German History Museum; Central Station.

tended for public officials. The last building in Berlin's new center, a multi-level central station, was completed in 2006 where the former Lehrter Stadtbahnhof stood.

Below right: Frederich the Great, completely restored, now rides again in the Forum Fridericianum, which has been rebuilt almost exactly to original plans. Eirene – renamed Victoria in 1814 – rides triumphant in her Quadriga atop the Brandenburg Gate (inset below). Indeed, after a peaceful revolution that reunited the two Germanies and the two Berlins, she is entitled to a victory lap.

HISTORIC MITTE

With the fall of the Wall on November 9, 1989, Berlin regained its historic center. Much of it had been destroyed during World War II and reconstructed during DDR times, but much of it still needed costly renovation. Today, the neoclassical grand boulevard Unter den Linden once again tells its tale of trial and tribulation over the centuries in both Berlin and Germany. The Nikolaiviertel has become a new Old Town, and the Museumsinsel, a World Heritage Sight, will remind us of glorious times in coming years.

The Brandenburger Tor has survived just about everything history has dealt it. Below, from top: Emperor Wilhelm II and his entourage saunter through the gate (around 1910). After World War II, the gate is damaged but still standing. The area around it and the glorious Quadriga were destroyed, however: Only one horse head remained and was taken to the Märkisches Museum. On August 13, 1961, the Gate found itself behind a stretch of the Wall at "the end of the world." Today, the Gate has been restored and the new Quadriga is visible from all sides.

Brandenburg Gate

Between 1788 and 1791, architect Carl Gotthard Langhans erected the crown jewel of the grand boulevard Unter den Linden: the Brandenburger Gate, a gateway into the historic city and a monument to the might of Prussia. Modelled on the propylaea monument of the Acropolis in Athens, the gate is a massive, austere sandstone edifice 26 m (85 ft) high and 65 m (215 ft) wide. Twelve Doric columns divide the double portico into five passages: the central one, 5.5 m (18 ft) wide, was reserved for the royal retinue, while the narrower passages were used by the infantry. The relief on top of the fascia depicts the gods of peace marching into the city; reliefs in the passages show the exploits of Hercules; and the gods Mars and Minerva guard the side wings. The Quadriga was created in 1789 to 1791, based on designs by sculptor Johann Gottfried Schadow.

The Brandenburg Gate has long been a popular backdrop for events (below): publicity stunts, Christopher Street Day, demonstrations against working conditions, the World Cup, the Love Parade and church congress (large picture). Hardly a day passes without some sort of activity here

(far right, from the top): Greenpeace protests nuclear power and harmful fishing practices; singers rehearse; Greenpeace battles nuclear power deals; and the German spirit of innovation is celebrated. In 2005, a massive screen showed the area at the end of World War II (right).

BRANDENBURGER TOR – ICON AND BACKDROP

Initially it was just a city gate, but again and again history rendered it a meaningful icon. in 1806, for example, after the French victory at Jena and Auerstedt, Napoleon I had the Quadriga packed into boxes and sent off to Paris. After German retribution at the Treaty of Paris in 1814, the goddess Victory was placed on Pariser Platz.

Traditionally, soldiers marched to war through the Brandenburg Gate and passed through it upon their return as well. On January 30, 1933, 25,000 uniformed followers of Adolf Hitler celebrated his appointment as Reich chancellor with a torchlit procession through the gate. The 85-year-old president of the Prussian

Academy of the Arts, Max Liebermann, once said his address was "immediately to the left of the Brandenburg Gate". After the war, the Gate was damaged, but it remained an icon of the city. On June 17, 1953, during the workers' uprising in East Berlin, locals hoisted the flag of West Germany here. When the Wall was built in

1961, the Brandenburger Tor came to symbolize the division, and when the country was reunified twenty-eight years later, it once again represented unity. Today, it bestows a special importance on every demonstration and every occasion that takes place here, and hardly a single day passes without some sort of event.

The Akademie der Künste on Pariser Platz: Walls tumble (below); catwalks criss-cross the interior (far right); behind the glass façade, the new building reveals traces of the old halls of the Akademie (right); superb views distract in the reading rooms (inset below).

Academy of Arts

The Academy of Arts in Berlin is no monotonous stone edifice but a glass façade behind which traces of the old Akademie der Künste are still visible. Architect Günter Behnisch fought long and hard to push his design through, campaigning tirelessly against erasing the real history in the district and adding to the mock-historical styles there. During the day, the façade reveals very little, reflecting the pompous stucco of the less attractive buildings that dominate Pariser Platz. Inside, however, everything is glass. There are no right angles. Is the building itself art? It has a surprisingly playful roof, where autumn leaves glow against the sky-blue. The new Akademie der Künste really comes alive at night, when it shines alone in a sea of sandstone façades and the warm light behind the glass front draws you to the slanted shapes inside.

Inset, from left: A bellhop opens the car door for guests, much like a hundred years ago. Calming music and a relaxing fountain welcome visitors in the spacious lobby after a day of sightseeing. People meet outside for coffee or a cocktail and enjoy the view of the Brandenburg Gate. Right: The new Hotel Adlon Kempinski Berlin, rebuilt in its old location, was intended to look just like in the "olden days". In fact, the Berlin Senate requested a replica, a building in the historicist style of the Wilhelminian era. Below: A view of the grand lobby at the Adlon.

HOTEL WITH TRADITION: THE ADLON

The German capital is certainly not lacking in five-star hotels, and new ones are still being built, but "the Adlon" was always something special. Emperor Wilhelm II called it a "temple of desires," and demanded that he be the first to step through the door when the hotel opened in 1907. The decadence begins right in the lobby, a combination of glitz and magical light – and money. Originally, there were baths and pleasant novelties such as tasselled bells to summon the staff. And of course the real fairy-tale story of the Adlon is that of the journeyman cabinet maker and showman Lorenz Adlon, who came from the city of Mainz, started as a builder, and went on to become owner of this elegant establishment. The hotel had actually more or less survived the aerial bombardments of World War II when, in May 1945, someone set fire to the wine cellars and destroyed the Berlin legend. After the fall of the Wall, a foundation was reset, and in 1996 the Adlon became the first building on Pariser Platz. It was to be boon for the cityscape as well as its 3,500 investors who had hoped the address would be Unter den Linden 1 (it turned out to be 77). Art critics revile the new Adlon's architecture, but Berliners and visitors seem to like it, not least because the light green copper roof is a good orientation in the city.

The large picture below shows the lights on Friedrichstrasse. Quartier 206 (right), with its angular oriel windows and façade that looks like origami, has a mysterious flare when lit up at night, while inside (far right), a bright marble mosaic twists and turns in a dizzying, Escher-like swirl. This is the most elegant part of an underground passage through three quarters, starting in the Galeries Lafayette food court. Here, an espresso is accompanied by relaxing piano music, and pale mannequins display expensive international designer wear.

Friedrichstraße

The best description was penned by columnist Franz Hessel in the early 20th century: "… the narrow pavement is covered by a carpet of light on which dangerous girls move as if on silk." He was talking about Friedrichstrasse, roughly from Unter den Linden to Leipziger Strasse, with its high-end restaurants and nightclubs, but also basement bars and gaming saloons. The lights have returned today, along with some elegant restaurants and expensive stores, the start of a new period of glitz that many had hoped for. But it is only on this central section of 3 km (2mi), from the Oranienburg Gate to Mehringplatz, that has fulfilled the lofty expectations of a new Berlin. When you reach Checkpoint Charlie, the new office blocks still stand empty, and yet, behind Friedrichstrasse station the contruction work continues.

Below: Jean Nouvel has arranged the levels of Galeries Lafayette around two spectacular glass cones. Swirling around the atrium, customers can admire the Frenchman's architecture while getting a bite to eat in the gourmet food court. People moving through the upper floors are silhouetted against the glass dome high above. Inside the store (insets right), luxury goods and the elegant creations of international designers are on display for more well-heeled clientele. Perhaps the diamond-encrusted dog collar will strike your animal-lover fancy.

SHOPPING IN BERLIN MITTE

Sunglasses displayed like jewels, fancy shoes adorning windows in stylish galleries, mirrors as tall as houses and bamboo plants on unrendered brick all draw curious passersby into the myriad stores, but the goods are only revealed once you enter. Shopping in Mitte is definitely entertaining, a pleasure for the senses and an aesthetic bonanza for connoisseurs. The large department stores of the prewar days have disappeared from the city center, except for the ones on Alexanderplatz. They have now been replaced by shopping malls like the ones on Potsdamer Platz. The boutiques that fill the historic Mitte are very often quite small, carefully laid out and very minimalist in style. They compete fiercely for the attention of would-be buyers with unique and flamboyant displays. And if that isn't enough to get your attention, there may be a DJ spinning records to provide customers with a soundtrack for their shopping spree. There may even be a show while a product is being crafted. Concept stores are a new departure in the overall consumer experience. Goods here satisfy more sophisticated tastes, from everyday household items to precious one-offs displayed in a variety of creative ways. You may find a pair of shoes, for example, presented with a piece of furniture that is also part of the deal.

Around the Gendarmenmarkt (below right) with its Konzerthaus, French cathedral and Schiller statue (below), life has always been on the more sophisticated side. Elegant establishments abound (right), such as the Borchardt, popular with politicians and media folk.

The Gendarmenmarkt

Gendarmenmarkt, with its ensemble of Schauspielhaus, German and French Doms (cathedrals), and the grand marble statue of the famous poet, Friedrich Schiller, is regarded as one of Berlin's most attractive squares and the pinnacle of romantic neoclassicism. Friedrich II had originally built the theater for comedy performances back in 1774, and the square itself is named after the Gens d'Armes, a regiment of cuirassiers. The Doms are named after the French word "dôme" for the cupolas on top of their identical towers. Friedrich II had commissioned Carl von Gontard to add the trademark cupola towers to the churches, which had been there since the early 18th century. Reinhold Begas' statue of Schiller, 6 m (20 ft) high, stands in front of the stairs, surrounded by philosophical and historical texts. It was removed in 1935 and returned its former spot in 1987.

Below: Inside the Konzerthaus, white, red and gold dominate the Renaissance décor. Renovations on the outside of the building began in 1984 according to original plans, but the DDR didn't need another theater so it was designated as a concert hall and remained one ever since.

The performances inside are very popular, and in summer the Konzerthaus also becomes a backdrop for open-air concerts (right). Since 1992, some 500,000 visitors have enjoyed more than 500 soloists, orchestras, bands, choirs and even ballet ensembles here.

KONZERTHAUS ON THE GENDARMENMARKT

The Konzerthaus has only been a concert hall since 1984. Originally, a French comedy theater had existed in this place in 1774, but from 1802 until 1817 the Deutsches Nationaltheater took over. Tragically, during a rehearsal in 1817, a curtain caught fire and the entire building burned down. Karl Friedrich Schinkel was then commissioned to design a replacement and between 1818 and 1821 he created Prussia's most modern theater. The main stairs to the lobby, with its glorious Ionic columns, was once reserved exclusively for the royal entourage. Even today, the theater is accessed from below the stairs. Most of the reliefs in the gables and the figures of the muses on the roof were created from designs by Schinkel. Apollo and his griffins on the roof were the work of Christian Daniel Rauch. The geniuses on panther and lion beside the stairs were the work of Christian Friedrich Tieck. The building was opened in 1821, with a performance of Goethe's *Iphigenia*, and the same year, Carl Maria von Weber's opera *Der Freischütz* premiered here. The playhouse became Germany's leading theater: in 1932, Gustaf Gründgens played Mephisto in Goethe's *Faust;* from 1934–1945, he was art director here; in 1945, at the end of the war, the SS set fire to the building; and in 1976, the DDR rebuilt it.

Behind hanging vines over the main entrance (right), the Staatsbibliothek houses roughly three million historic volumes (below). The collection dates from 1501 to 1945 and is listed in catalogue boxes. The 200,000 rare books may only be viewed here.

Staatsbibliothek

In 1661, the Great Elector Friedrich Wilhelm laid the cornerstone for what is now the most important general library of science in Germany. Until 1701, the library was located in the pharmacy wing of the palace, but was moved to the "Kommode" on Bebelplatz where it became the Prussian State Library. During World War II, the books were kept safe in thirty different monasteries, castles and mines. Some returned to the house at Unter den Linden No. 8, but the majority went to a new building on Potsdamer Strasse in West Berlin. In 1992, the roughly ten million books, journals, manuscripts and cartographic works were brought together once again. Today, it is a research library for pre-1955 literature. While it was still the Academy of Sciences, controversial philosopher Johann Gottlieb Fichte made some legendary speeches from the Roter Saal (red room) here.

At the Humboldt University, teaching and research have always adapted to the times. The former royal residence has experienced several radical changes in its history, as is evident from Karl Marx's maxim in the entrance hall (below). Alexander von Humboldt (right), brother of the university's founder and a natural scientist who spent his life doing research in Central and South America, might not have agreed with Marx. Either way, the computers in the grand halls designed by Knobelsdorff in the 18th century (far right) certainly seem out of place.

Die Philosophen haben nur verschieden inter es kommt aber dara sie zu verändern

Humboldt University

Humboldt University, known until 1946 as Friedrich Wilhelm University, can be proud of its history: It has produced twenty-nine Nobel Prize winners, among them Albert Einstein (physics), Otto Hahn (chemistry), Robert Koch (medicine) and Theodor Mommsen (literature). Above these famous figures, Alexander von Humboldt and his brother Wilhelm stand guard over the Forum Fridericianum where rare gingko trees grow in the garden. Constructed from 1748 to 1765 by Johann Bouman, the building was originally destined for Prince Heinrich, Friedrich II' brother. Since he rarely made use of it, however, Wilhelm von Humboldt proposed a university and philosopher Johann Gottlieb Fichte became its first director in 1810. Among its teachers were Hegel, the brothers Grimm, Planck, Virchow and Sauerbruch. Karl Marx also studied here from 1836 to 1841.

die Welt
retiert.
an,

Karl Marx

Below: Enlarged to four times her original size, the *Mother and Her Dead Son*, a bronze pietà by Käthe Kollwitz, still appears very small kneeling in the center of the floor in the Neue Wache. From 1816 to 1818, Karl Friedrich Schinkel built a small neoclassical temple with Doric columns in a chestnut glade, where previously an artillery guard house had protected the former palace. It was Schinkel's first public commission and soon became a prototype for his classicism, which to this day characterizes a large portion of historic Berlin (right).

Neue Wache

Since 1993, the Neue Wache (new guard house) has been the principal memorial in Germany for victims of war and dictatorship. After World War I, it became the memorial for those who had died in that war. From 1951 to 1957, the GDR renovated the building, which had been destroyed during World War II. After 1962, the memorial for victims of fascism and militarism became a magnet for photographers during the weekly changing of the GDR guards who goose-stepped in Prussian style through the process. In 1969, the DDR regime even changed the inside of Schinkel's guard house by adding a crystal cube with an eternal flame and urns with the ashes of the unknown resistance soldier. The vaults underneath two bronze plates contained "the blood-drenched soil from fascist concentration camps" and other battlefields.

After reunification, the Zeughaus (right) became the Deutsches Historisches Museum. The historic courtyard (below) now has a glass roof and serves as a concert venue in summer. After extensive reconstruction, the permanent display (far right) includes a prayer book from the Meissen diocese in Leipzig from 1519) with an altar picture from about 1485; Duke Friedrich II's equestrian armor from Liegnitz, Brieg and Wohlau and a 16th-century battle harness; historic costumes; an antiaircraft gun from World War II as well as a classic VW Beetle.

Zeughaus

The oldest structure on the boulevard Unter den Linden that is still preserved today was orignally built between 1695 and 1706 as an arsenal, and it was used as such until the 19th century. It was stormed once more during the 1848 Revolution. The original architects, Nering and Grünberg, retired early and left the completion of the project to Andreas Schlüter. Already busy working on the palace, Schlüter's main contributions to the stoic edifice were its decorative sculptures. His masterpiece can be admired in the inner courtyard, above the cap stones of the window arches: relief sculptures of twenty-two heads of dying soldiers. The Zeughaus, complemented by a new wing built by Chinese-American architect Leoh Ming Pei, is today the German History Museum and contains several rare items such as Frederich the Great's camp bed.

The Deutsche Staatsoper (below) was completely rebuilt between 1951 to 1955. Steffi Scherzer, the prima ballerina, performed there until 2003 (far right). The Kronprinzenpalais (right) had to be reconstructed from old engravings.

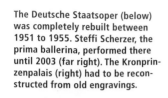

FRIDERICVS REX APOLLINI

MDCCXLII

Deutsche Staatsoper, Kronprinzenpalais

Both of these buildings were important at different times in their histories: the Staatsoper (state opera house) began as part of young King Friedrich II's dream of a Forum Fridericianum – a place of cultural enlightenment to unite the sciences, arts and the monarchy – and this was to be the first step, a "magical palace", an opera house. Designed by Georg Wenzeslaus von Knobelsdorff around 1741, it was the first theater in Germany that was not inside a royal palace. In 1789, it was opened to the "general" public, but the complex was never actually completed. The Kronprinzenpalais, built in 1663 and remodelled several times since, was initially important as the prince's city residence, but was later a guesthouse for state visitors to the GDR. On August 31, 1990, the two Germanies signed their Unification Treaty in its Roter Saal (red room).

The neoclassical Altes Museum is Karl Friedrich Schinkel's masterpiece and completes the north side of the Lustgarten (below). Eighteen Ionic columns carry the impressive, 87-m (285-ft) wide entablature. Only after the master builder's death – and deviating from his design – were statues positioned on either side of the stairs, including *Amazon Fighting with the Tiger* by August Kiss (right). Until the completion of the Neues Museum, the busts, the beautiful head of Nefertiti and the sarcophagi are temporary exhibits from the Egyptian Museum (insets).

Altes Museum, Neues Museum

Even when it was built in 1823, the Altes Museum (Old Museum), was more than just a gallery – it is the most important example of neoclassical architecture in Berlin. Karl Friedrich Schinkel, the museum's architect, managed to create a bourgeoisie meeting point in the midst of a monarchical society near both the palace and the arsenal. A wide flight of stairs leads to the columned hall modelled on Ancient Greece. The rotunda inside is encircled by sculptures and is reminiscent of the Pantheon in Rome. The collections that Friedrich Wilhelm III bought for the gallery formed the basis for Berlin's state museums of Prussian heritage. After years of renovation, the Neues Museum promises to be extraordinary, but Friedrich August Stüler's masterpiece, with artistic cast-iron elements, ceiling hangings and a vast collection of paintings, could only be very minimally preserved.

Below: The Pergamon Altar is a big draw for visitors along with the Ishtar Gate (far right), the Processional Way from Babylon, and the Market Gate of Miletus (insets). Also on display are sculptures from Miletus, Samos and Naxos (right). At bottom left is the Propylon to Athena.

Pergamon Museum

Berlin's most exciting steps take you past giants and gods to the Pergamon Altar where sacrifices were made over 2,000 years ago in Ancient Greece. The altar, which had been built in about 180–160 BC, was excavated in 1902 by Carl Humann and moved to Berlin. This offering from King Eumenes to (presumably) Zeus and Athena, patron goddess of the town of Pergamon (present-day Bergama in Turkey), was to be put on display, and so the first architecture museum in the world was built between 1909–1930 according to plans by Alfred Messel and Ludwig Hoffmann. Today it is the most-visited museum in Berlin. In the basement of the Pergamon is a collection of antiquities from Asia Minor containing finds from 4,000 years of art, mostly excavated by the German Orient Society between 1898 and 1917, as well as items relating to Asian history and culture.

The ensemble of art at the Skulp-turensammlung (sculpture collection) and the Museum für Byzantinische Kunst (Byzantine art) have now been reunited after being separated since 1939, and a dome once again crowns the impressive edifice (right). The small hall below the cupola (below), with its opulent rococo staircase, is a dedication to Frederic the Great as well as a gallery for the most famous sculptors who worked in Berlin between 1750 to 1800. The dome itself is richly segmented, the walls are made from cast stone and the banisters are gilded.

Bode Museum

The neo-baroque Bode Museum juts into the Spree river near the Monbijou Bridge like the bow of a ship. Designed by Ernst von Ihne and opened in 1904 as the Kaiser Friedrich Museum, it was renamed in 1956 to honour its first director, Wilhelm von Bode. The stunning building features a basilica, cupola halls, statues of princes, and Italian fireplaces. After its destruction, the museum required a near complete rebuilding to regain its original aura. The four-way segmentation of the dome and the vaulted ceiling have been reconstructed, flooding the hall with light, and the inlaid marble in the basilica has been renovated. Even Tiepolo's cabinet and the frescoes are back on display. The coin collection, the museum of Byzantine art und the sculpture collection, with its 1,700 pieces dating from late antiquity to the end of the 18th century, are all housed here now.

In summer, the garden of the Alte Nationalgalerie hosts a variety of open-air events such as film screenings and concerts. From high up in the gables, statues by Rudolf Schweinitz symbolizing the three disciplines of painting, sculpture and architecture stand guard over the scene.

Inside, Christian Friedrich Tieck's bust of Karl Friedrich Schinkel stands next to a copy by Wilhelm Ahlborns of Schinkel's painting (right) *Blick in Griechenlands Blüte* (*Greece's in its Prime*). The original went missing. Right and top: Sculptures and paintings keep your attention.

Alte Nationalgalerie

The Alte Nationalgalerie (old national gallery) stands like a Corinthian temple on massive raised base. Karl Friedrich Schinkel's pupil, Friedrich August Stüler, designed the building in 1865, and it was completed with the help of bourgeois sponsorship. In his will, Consul Wagner gave 262 paintings to the Prussian prince regent, which were to be exhibited in a national gallery. At beginning of the 20th century, the directors rejected his overwhelmingly "Wilhelminian" tastes, buying instead works by Manet, Monet and Menzel. In 1939, the exhibition was declared "degenerate art" by the Nazis and closed down. After World War II, the gallery was one of the first on Museum Island to be rebuilt, and between 2001 it was complete renovated. Great 19th-century works from the likes of Caspar David Friedrich, Max Liebermann and Lovis Corinth are once again on display.

Even in winter, the evening sun bathes the grey stone of the Berliner Dom (cathedral) in a warm light (right). In 2005, on the 100th anniversary of its consecration, light installation artist Matthias Zeckert created a splendid display, illuminating like candles the mighty sand- stone pillars and columns that support the cupola. Crowned by the Reformers like blazing flames (inset), before being drenched in a heavenly blue (far right). Even the dark wood of the fabulous organ and its 113 registers and more than 7,200 pipes were brightly lit (below).

The Berliner Dom

The burial church of the Hohenzollerns was erected on the order of Emperor Wilhelm II in 1893, on the site of an earlier court chapel. This "Principal Church of Prussian Protestantism" was to be lavishly designed in the style of the Italian High Renaissance, loaded with turrets and cupolas. Ultimately, it was built next to the Spree based oncontroversial designs by architect and master builder Julius Carl Raschdorff. The architect had simply selected features from various handbooks of architecture and plans of dozens of historical buildings, creating a cathedral reminiscent of London and Rome, of famous palaces and well-known temples. The real treasures of the burial church are in its vaults: ninety-four tombs and sarcophagi of the former ruling dynasty spanning four centuries. The cathedral has always remained a royal chapel, and was never the bishop's mother church.

In 1993/1994, a painted façade showed Berliners and visitors what it would have looked like if the Hohenzollern palace in the middle of the city had been rebuilt. The printed canvas was an appeal to reconstruct the palace and invited new members of the association set up to promote it. It displayed original reliefs and sculptures stored at Hohenschönhausen (far right), hoping to raise funds for the reconstruction. However, the demolition of the Palast der Republik (right), which occupied only part of the former palace's grounds, still upset most Berliners.

FROM PALAST DER REPUBLIK TO STADTSCHLOSS

At the end of World War II, only thirteen of sixty-nine buildings were still standing between the palace and Pariser Platz. The DDR rebuilt many of these, but not the palace. In 1950, using 13 tons of explosives, the partially destroyed Hohenzollern Stadtschloss (city palace) was finally demolished as "historical trash". A structure that had first been built as a castle for Elector Friedrich II in 1443–1451, and enlarged and remodelled over the centuries, thus became a veritable museum of architecture. In 1973–1976, the Palast der Republik was built as a grand edifice on the Spree, with a mirror façade and numerous halls, according to plans by Heinz Graffunder, and was the seat of the Volkskammer (parliament). Because of its many lights, it soon became known as "Erichs Lampenladen" (Erich [Honecker]'s lighting store), or "Palazzo Prozzo" (swank palace), but it was still visited often by Berliners. As early as September 1990, it was closed because of asbestos contamination, but it was refurbished, and finally demolished in 2006. In 2002, after heavy debate, parliament had voted to rebuild the city palace as the Humboldt Forum, a building to accommodate all the museums currently based at Dahlem. Until there is sufficient money to realize the project, however, the area will probably be remain a green space.

The Nikolai district is recognizable by the two towers of the Nikolai church, which are unusual in Berlin (far right), and the TV tower reveals the area's proximity to Alexanderplatz (below and right). The Baltic Sea gables (right) show the scarcity of construction materials back then.

Nikolai District

A church on the site of an earlier, probably 12th-century house of worship; a stretch of medieval town wall with the city's first tavern; and the ruins of a monastery are all remains of old Berlin here in the Nikolai district. The ford on the Spree river was already settled 800 years ago, and today it is a busy main road. Those in search of the old town in the Nikolaiviertel will be happy to find a heritage theme park here as well. Because very little sur-

vived World War II, the East Berlin magistrate had everything rebuilt in 1987, for Berlin's 750th anniversary: original houses were brought in, others were reconstructed in precast concrete with Rostock-style gables, and all were decorated in nostalgic style and some 780 new apartment buildings were erected. The former Marienviertel is now a spacious but anonymous square with the Marien church, a fountain and the TV tower.

The Berlin town hall owes its name to the red bricks used in its construction (below), not to the political persuasion of the ruling party. The 94-m (308-ft) clocktower is of course dwarfed by the TV tower, but the square in front of the Rathaus (below) is adorned with the impressive Neptune fountain, built by Reinhold Begas in 1891. The fountain once stood between the Stadtschloss and the Marstall. Reminiscent of Berni-ni's Fountain of the Four Rivers in Rome, Neptune is surrounded by the Elbe, Weichsel, Oder and the Rhine in this sculpture.

Rotes Rathaus

After an interruption of fifty-eight years, Berlin's municipal council once again moved into the Rotes Rathaus in 1991. Since then it has been functioning as town hall for the entire city. The council had been deprived of its power back in 1933, although the red-brick building had always been regarded as a symbol of the confident citizen. Built between 1860 and 1869 by Hermann Friedrich Waesemann with Italian High Renaissance influences, the façade decoration documents the history of the city since its foundation in the 13th century. A frieze consisting of thirty-six terracotta plaques runs around the building underneath the windows of the main floor, presenting the so-called "stone chronicle." Allegorical statues on the stairs depict navigation, agriculture, fishing and trade, and the windows of the crest hall are adorned with the crests of all of Berlin's districts.

Berlin's iconic TV tower, which can be seen for miles, becomes the central focus when seen through the Weltzeituhr (world time clock) on Alexanderplatz (below). Marx and Engels, with the Spree river behind them, stare stoicly at the tower (far right). The collage at right shows a panorama view of what is actually far apart for a pedestrian: Karl-Liebknecht-Strasse, which runs alongside Alexanderplatz; the vast Alexanderplatz itself; and the TV tower and the Marienkirche opposite the Rotes Rathaus, like something from long forgotten days.

Marx Engels Forum, Alexanderplatz

The real heart of Berlin is difficult to pin down: the TV tower and Marienkirche stand on a square without a name; to the southwest, towards the Spree, is the expansive Marx Engels Forum; nearby in the northeast is Alexanderplatz. Since 1986, Engels has stood here, larger than life, next to the seated Marx, and surrounded by metal columns that document the history of class struggle. Where once a maze of alleyways surrounded the Marienkirche, which dates back to 1270, the TV tower now dominates at 368 m (1,207 ft). If you want, you can have take the high-speed elevator to the viewing platform in 40 seconds. Once the cattle market outside the Oderberg Gate, Alexanderplatz was renamed in 1805 after the Russian Tsar Alexander I. Not much of it remained after the war, so new houses line the square and, thus far, plans for high-rises have been put on ice.

Brightly painted brickwork is a delightful effect even at night, as can be seen in the picture below. This is what August Endell set out to show with his design "the beauty of large cities." In the Hackesche Höfe (far right) you can drink a coffee and shop till you drop. Right: Fascinating red, blue and yellow light installations in the Sophie Gips Höfe, where once gypsum and later sewing machines were manufactured before an artistic transformation created an entirely new look. The Rosenhöfe, with their playful balustrades, keep visitors entertained.

Hackesche Höfe

From the outside you see nothing. The plaster was removed as early as 1961. But once you step inside the courtyards on Rosenthaler Strasse, you will be greeted by an extraordinary scene: tiles fired based on historic models and glazed in golden, blue and green hues are arranged in dynamic patterns while elegant windows and curved rooflines keep people's attention. Avant-garde artist, August Endell, was commissioned with the design in 1906, and wanted to create something new in place of the heavily Wilhelminian art scene. He ultimately added magic to what was already a sensation in the early 20th century, and proprietor Kurt Berndt built the largest interconnecting complex of homes and buildings in Europe, with eight courtyards. The economy boomed, property prices were rising and here, both homes and studios were built simultaneously in the courtyards.

Berlin has a style for everyone, whether you are seeking a more concealing look, as in Islamic fashion, or more revealing, as in the lingerie store (right). Vivienne Westwood, one of the UK's most famous fashion designers, is a professor in Berlin and encourages her students at the University of the Arts to be creative. When the graduating class finally presents its designs on the catwalk (below), it is the climax after a hard year of studies. Before the great moment, make-up, haircut and last stitches are all part of the preparations (insets below).

BERLIN'S "YOUNG FASHION"

Berlin fashion? Isn't that something like track suit bottoms, balloon silk, and maybe gold buttons or an open shirt? Well, not anymore. It's been a while since people laughed at those stereotypes. Young fashion designers from Berlin now present their collections in Tokyo and New York. Designers from Finland and England sell their creations in small stores in Prenzlauer Berg. Fiona Bennet, originally a hatmaker, is known for unique creations. Zeha exclusive sneakers are hailed as a combination of nostalgia and cool, yet they are revival GDR. Berlin labels adorn spectacles, handbags and shoes now. Annual shows like "Walk of Fashion" and "Bread & Butter", Bare are considered contemporary and even visionary, while the "Premium" trend show for upmarket street couture attracts buyers and sellers from Germany and abroad. In 1900, the trade magazine Der Confektionär reported, "the history of fashion in Berlin is also the history of the fashion industry in Germany, which was the first to conquer a global market." As early as 1288, when Berlin was still but a village, Berlin tailors set themselves up as an official guild. Today there are seven schools of fashion in the city, as well as a multitude of small, elegant boutiques throughout the city, in Mitte and Prenzlauer Berg, in Charlottenburg and in Kreuzberg …

The cornerstone for the reconstruction of Berlin's destroyed synagogue was laid in November 1988, and on May 7, 1995, the Jewish community of Berlin celebrated its consecration. From the outside, the building looks exactly as it did in the 19th century (below). The gilded cupola gleams once again in the sunshine (right), but once you push open the heavy doors (far right), you no longer enter a place of worship. Today, there is only a small prayer room, while all the other rooms are used for cultural events and conferences, as well as for a permanent exhibition.

The New Synagogue

Golden domes dominate Berlin's inner city skyline. Inspired by the Alhambra in Spain, Eduard Knobloch began construction of the original synagogue in 1859, and it was completed by Schinkel's pupil August Stüler in 1866. At the time, the Neue Synagoge was a self-confident expression of an established Jewish community: organ music, a mixed choir and prayers in German were commonplace in the reform community. In September 1930, Albert Einstein played concerts by Bach and Händel. A courageous policeman managed to save the Moorish work of art from destruction by the SA on November 9, 1938, but a British air raid in 1943 left the synagogue in ruins. Today, the Jewish community again invites guests to its Centrum Judaicum. An exhibition explores everyday Jewish life before the war, and conveys much of the former vibrancy of this district.

Behind the Philharmonie (below, foreground) and the Matthäus-Kirche (far right) rises the canopy roof of the Sony Center (middle), the TV tower (background) and Debis City (right). The Gemälde-galerie (inset below), is home to more than 900 European paintings, making it one of the most valuable collections in the world.

NEW MITTE
GOVERNMENT DISTRICT, TIERGARTEN, POTSDAMER PLATZ

Who still remembers the Wall and the Hasenwiese, or a lonely house on Potsdamer Platz, which actually hasn't been a platz (square) for ages? Out of the largest building site the western world has seen in decades has risen a highly modern district, full of architectural treats and surprises. Only a short walk from the Tiergarten, brand-new parliamentary buildings are connected by bridges over the Spree. The Reichstag building, with its glass dome, and the Holocaust memorial also draw scores of visitors to the "new" Mitte.

The pictures to the right and far right show the present-day Reichstag building (parliament). Below, from top: Opening of the Reichstag by the emperor in 1888; interior and façade of the new building in 1894; in 1938, Hitler's Field Marshall Göring presided here; on May 2, 1945, Red Army soldiers hoisted the Soviet flag over the ruins.

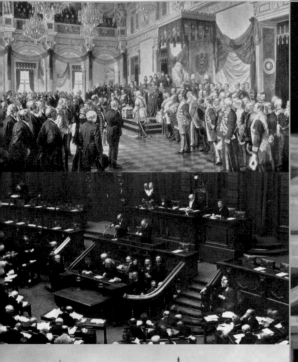

Reichstag Building

Traffic signs lead the way to the Reichstag building (parliament), where hundreds visitors stand in line each day to get a glimpse of the modernized edifice. Built between 1884 and 1894, by Paul Wallot, it was meant to symbolize the grandeur and might of the German empire, but Emperor Wilhelm II regarded the building as "the peak of bad taste." The inscription, "To the German People," was only added in 1916, during World War I.

Damaged in World War II, the building was restored as a conference venue in 1961, and in 1995, artist Christo and his wife Jeanne Claude wrapped the building in silvery fabric. Behind the historic façade of the Reichstag, an environmentally-friendly and modern government facility has now been built based on plans by Lord Foster but, as in the Wallot project over one hundred years ago, the glass dome was once again controversial.

Visitors have access to the roof and the dome of the Reichstag building (below) nearly every day of the year, from morning to midnight. Those who get there early won't have to wait long. In the evening (right), the surrounding buildings are first transformed into silhouettes against the colorful twilight, then the massive expanse of the Tiergarten disappears, and finally, a new look for the city is conjured up by the lights of the offices and stores, countless street lamps, headlights from traffic and the brightly lit S-Bahn trains rolling by above the sparkling Spree.

LORD FOSTER'S DOME

The glass dome of the Reichstag building towers 23.5 m (77 ft) above its visitors, and has a diameter of 40 m (131 ft). The view from the roof terrace includes the Kanzleramt (chancellery) in a bend on the Spree as well as other new parliamentary buildings. At the base of the dome is an exhibit with the building's history, and from the roof terrace you can begin the 230-m (251-yds) climb up the spiralling ramps, which take you to the top of the dome at a constant eight-degree grade. What looks like a giant reflective wheel hub that visitors walk around, is in fact the ventilation shaft of the plenary chamber. Thermal uplift allows the depleted air to funnel upwards and out of the crown of the dome. Precisely 360 mirrors direct daylight down into the plenary chamber, which lies 10 m (33 ft) below, and a sophisticated computer system adjusts them over the course of the day to ensure that the sun does not blind the delegates in the hall below. The glass panes, covering an area of 3,000 sq m (32,280 sq ft), overlap like scales on the central column. Each day, sand, dust and wind make the mirrors less reflective, and window cleaners come to maintain them. For a few days then, visitors are not allowed to watch the delegates from the roof. Only those who wish to go to the rooftop restaurant are still allowed up there during that period.

Daylight from the cupola roof (right) engulfs parliamentary delegates below. Only the seats of the backbenchers are overshadowed by the visitor catwalks. When asked for proposals, architect Lord Foster sketched nearly a thousand designs for a federal eagle. Not one of them was approved, so the old "fat hen" from Bonn, a shiny aluminum eagle, was brought to parliament as the heraldic animal (inset below). The delegates' actual discussions take place in the Paul-Löbe-Haus on the opposite bank of the Spree (below).

THE GERMAN BUNDESTAG

Eight years passed between June 20, 1991, when parliament decided to make Berlin the seat of the Bundestag, and April 19, 1999, when the entire German parliament had its first session in the Reichstag building. The vote was ultimately decided by a narrow but sufficient majority of eighteen. In July 1995, renovations began, and an English architect experienced German democracy at work. The jury found it difficult to decide among the international design entries, and finally awarded not just one but three first prizes. In the end, renowned architect, Lord Foster, convinced the Bundestag with his plans for how the space should be used, and was awarded the contract to design an entirely new facility inside the old shell. Workers shifted some 45,000 tons of rubble from inside the building, until only the outer shell and some load-bearing interior walls remained of the old Wallot structure. Red Army graffiti from May 1945 was found and partially preserved. Foster positioned the glass plenary chamber, which measures 1,200 sq m (12,912 sq ft) and extends over three floors, in the center of the building. Twelve thin, 22-m-long (72-ft) columns carry the dome above the chamber. As in the historic Reichstag, delegates are seated facing east. Visitors reach the stands in the plenary hall via a mezzanine floor.

In the courtyard of the federal chancellery on the Spree (right), is the sculpture *Unity* by Eduardo Chillida. It appears light but Basque blacksmiths shaped the 90 tons into a 5-m-wide (16-ft), 6-m-high (20-ft) structure (below). Among the works of art here, the building houses the gallery of chancellors (insets below, from left): Konrad Adenauer (by H.J. Kallmann), Ludwig Erhard (G. Rittner), Kurt Georg Kiesinger (G. Rittner), Willy Brandt (O. Petersen), Helmut Schmidt (B. Heisig), Helmut Kohl (A. Gehse), and Gerhard Schröder (Jörg Immendorf).

Federal Chancellery

Berliners have nicknamed the Bundeskanzleramt (federal chancellery) the "washing machine." The angular cube measures 55 m (180 ft) down each side and has two symmetric 21-m-wide (69-ft) wings. It has 300 offices on five floors, all of them measuring 20 sq m (215 sq ft) and facing the Spree. Since April 30, 2001, the official address of the chancellor's office has been No. 1 Willy-Brandt-Strasse. In just four years, 230 million euros were spent on the project. Locals are not sure how, but sometimes they watch from behind a fence when state visitors are welcomed in the courtyard. A wide staircase in the lobby provides a grand setting for photo calls. The office of the chancellor occupies 145 sq m (1,560 sq ft) on the seventh floor, where the chancellor enjoys views of the Reichstag and the Brandenburg Gate through windows secured with 8-cm-thick (5-cm) bullet-proof glass.

In 1871, the Lehrter Bahnhof (right) was opened where today the Hauptbahnhof stands on the Spree. From here, the "Flying Hamburger" reaches that Hanseatic city in just over two hours and eighteen minutes. Glass panes form a vault above the upper hall of the new central station (top inset and main picture). The Hamburg trains, however, depart from the lower level, which has a flat ceiling (bottom inset).

Central Station (Lehrter Bahnhof)

A truly superlative central train station was put into operation in Berlin on May 28, 2006: the largest interchange station in Europe, fitted with the most extensive photovoltaic system in Europe, and featuring 78,000 solar cells, 1,200 loudspeakers, 203 video cameras, six panoramic lifts, forty-three ordinary lifts and fifty-four escalators. The S-Bahn trains on Level 2 and the platform for the trains to Munich on Level -2 are actually separated by three floors spanning 25 m (82 ft). A vault of 8,000 glass panes covers the upper hall at a height of 321 m (1,053 ft), with 85 km (53 miles) of steel cable for stability. The arches were assembled as towers and lowered into place. No one disputes the 700 million euros spent, but it is not only the station that is new to the city. For one hundred years, Berlin has dreamt of a north-south link – now it has become a reality.

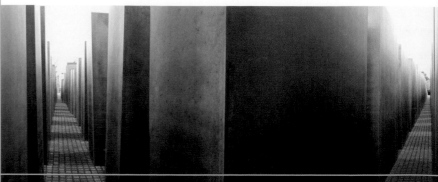

Every day, roughly 10,000 people walk through the concrete steles of the memorial (right and below), which at first glance appears quite unspectacular. But as you get closer, they are like a slowly moving sea of stones. Inside, the waves change size as the pillars range in height from a hand's width up to almost 5 m (16 ft) and the paths rise and fall at random. The sun casts shadows of different lengths. At night, some experience a sense of security while others find the darkness sinister. The visitor center confronts you with real faces (insets).

Holocaust Memorial

It was controversial: a walkable stone field near the Brandenburg Gate consisting of 2,711 dark concrete pillars of varying sizes, placed along irregular, narrow passages, open day and night. Architect Peter Eisenman broke with the customary symbolism for memorials. Visitors have to find their own way into and out of the memorial while facing their own thoughts and feelings. Important facts about the holocaust and extermination camps await you in the subterranean information center where visitors are then confronted with the real stories. You can read accounts of persecution in the Raum der Familien (room of families) and get a look at the different lives of fifteen European Jews before the war. In the Raum der Namen (room of names), the names and brief biographies of murdered and missing Jews are read aloud.

Established as a party area after various Love Parades (below), New Year's Eve celebrations and the 2006 World Cup, the Tiergarten on either side of the Strasse des 17. Juni remains first and foremost a place of relaxation, with statues, bridges and tranquil sanctuaries (far right).

Visitors can climb up 285 steps in the Siegessäule (below) at Grosser Stern, to just below the flowing robes of Eirene, the goddess of victory by Friedrich Drake (right, with Bismarck statue). From the viewing platform at 48-m (157-ft), the sea of trees is an impressive sight.

Tiergarten, Siegessäule, Strasse des 17. Juni

It begins at the Brandenburg Gate, or near Potsdamer Platz: a 3-km-wide (2-mile) and 1-km-long (1,093-yd) forest park in the middle of the city, with the Neuer See (new lake) at its center. In 2006, it was enlarged by a further 45,000 sq m (484,200 sq ft) to cover an area where a relief road served as north-south-axis after the Wall was demolished. That road has been replaced by the Tiergarten tunnel. Until the 16th century, the forest was fenced in as the electors' hunting ground before a leisure park was finally installed by Friedrich II with footpaths, statues and labyrinths. Eirene, the 8-m (26-ft) statue of the goddess of victory atop the Siegessäule (victory column), commemorates three victories: against Denmark (1864), Austria (1866) and France (1870/1871). The Street of June 17th cuts through the Grosser Stern (great star) roundabout and the Tiergarten.

The German president invites his guests to the former royal palace (below). The interior (right) contains a modest office, a salon with hardwood floors and abstract paintings, and the oval Langhans room.

Schloss Bellevue

Completed in 1785, this palace was Prussia's first neo-classical building. It has had a remarkable career since then: from royal summer residence to, since 1994, the home of the German president. Michael Philipp Daniel Bouman originally designed the summer palace for Prince August Ferdinand of Prussia, Friedrich II's youngest brother. Emperor Wilhelm II made it the venue for consultations with his army commanders. In 1928, Bellevue became the property of the state, and in 1935, it was made into the Museum of German Ethnography. The next transformation came in 1938, when it was a guesthouse for Third Reich leaders. When Bonn was still the federal capital, Bellevue was the West Berlin residence where even the furnishing was a topic for debate: "Empire 1959" is how the critics reviled the gilded ceilings and curved lounge chairs, but all that has been forgotten.

The slim light shafts on Potsdamer Strasse (below) shine daylight into the Potsdamer Platz subway station. They look so much like artworks that passersby rarely notice that they actually have a function. To get them all in focus was not easy for the photographer. Seen from the air, you can make out various buildings on the square (right): in the foreground are the Beisheim Center and the Ritz Carlton Hotel; left is the red Kollhoff Haus, with an excellent view of the city from its golden battlements; and to the right is the round structure of the Sony Center.

Potsdamer Platz

It hasn't actually been a Platz, or square, for a long time Rather, it is a new district located in the former no-man's land between East and West Berlin, with luxury apartments, offices, hotels, cinemas and restaurants. What was once Europe's largest urban building site has now given rise to the designs of internationally renowned architects like Renzo Piano, Richard Rogers, Arata Isozaki, Hans Kollhoff, Helmut Jahn and Giorgio Grassi who combined to create a truly 21st-century cityscape that is both admired and criticized in equal measures. The cornerstone was laid in October 1994; in 1996, Daniel Barenboim conducted dancing cranes for the topping-out ceremony; in 1998, ten roads and seventeen buildings were opened. In December 2000, the red Info-box, which gave visitors a glimpse of the construction site, was auctioned off, piece by piece.

The first impression of the Sony Center is overwhelming (below). Its canopy roof is an extensive avant-garde structure (insets), inside which everything reflects everything, creating a world of illusions in the Filmmuseum or in the subterranean cinemas (right).

Sony Center

Sony Center

Architect Helmut Jahn's answer to the stone Daimler Areal was a complex made of glass and steel. The buildings of his structure encircle a courtyard above which a spectacular roof is anchored to a steel ring frame and suspended with cables. The fabric canopy, which can be illuminated at night, protects the Urban Entertainment Center below with its cinemas, restaurants and cafés. A second engineering masterpiece is hidden inside the landmark rooms: Kaisersaal (emperor's chamber) and the Frühstückssaal (breakfast room) of the former luxury hotel Esplanade, dating from 1911. In yet another spectacular feat of engineering, the former, weighing 1,300 tons, was actually moved 75 m (246 ft) on air cushions in 1996. To avoid any damage to the antique chamber, the architect suspended it from above by a bridge-like support.

Every year, the Musical Theater on Potsdamer Platz is transformed into the Berlinale Palast for the opening of the film festival (far right). The crush of spectators is massive for both film screenings, which are open to visitors from around the world, and the arrival of the film stars at the opening ceremony (right). Below: In 2003, Richard Gere, Catherine Zeta-Jones, Renée Zellweger, Rob Marshall and Jon C. Reilly presented themselves on the red carpet for hundreds of photographers, who certainly enjoyed the opportunity.

Berlinale Palast

BERLIN FILM FESTIVAL

The 50th International Film Festival in Berlin (the Berlinale) in February 2000, was a very special event indeed. For the first time, the red carpet was rolled out on the brand-new Potsdamer Platz, while people around the square were still standing in the mud. The Musical Theater was officially declared a film palace and the movie stars returned after shying away for years from the dreary Berlin February. And this time not just to carry home their 4-kg (9-lb) Berlin Bear, the film festival award designed by sculptor Renée Sintenis. It was truly a new beginning. It was here fourteen years earlier that Wim Wenders shot his film *Wings of Desire* and asked 86-year-old Curt Bois to be part of it. Curt's famous reply to showing up at the then non-descript location: "I can't find Potsdamer Platz." The festival began in 1951 as the IFB, Internationale Filmfestspiele Berlin, before being renamed the Berlinale, an idea from cabaret artist Tatjana Sais, a member of the original jury. The Allied culture attachés promoted the new event, which featured imported films and foreign stars, to entertain the local population of the war-torn city. It wasn't until later that the Berlinale, held then in the Zoopalast in West Berlin, emerged as serious competition for the film festivals of Venice and Cannes. Nonetheless, it has always been a glamorous event.

The Philharmonie shines golden (right) amidst the otherwise unspectacular Kulturforum. Acoustic sails ensure perfect sound above the terraced hall (below). The interior of the Gemäldegalerie, outwardly unremarkable, houses myriad surprises for visitors (inset).

Kulturforum, Philharmonie

The Kulturforum and its museums – Neue Nationalgalerie, Gemäldegalerie, Kupferstichkabinett, Kunstgewerbe- und Musikinstrumentenmuseum – seem modest in their as yet unfinished state. Only the Philharmonie, designed by Hans Scharoun and built in 1960–1963 next to the Kammermusiksaal, warrants a second look – although the real experience here is of course inside. In the middle of the building is the orchestra platform, surrounded by seats for 2,200 spectators. It looks at once playful and severe, and the acoustics below the suspended roof sails are superb. Connoisseurs wax lyrical about the incomparable sound of the Berlin Philharmonic Orchestra, conducted by Sir Simon Rattle. But even those who do not have a special affinity to symphonic concerts can enjoy the superb sound – Juliette Gréco has appeared here, as has Hildegard Knef.

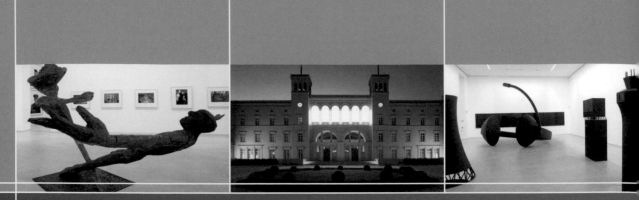

Art of the 20th century: Henry Moore's *The Archer* in front of the Neue Nationalgalerie (below); the Picasso exhibition (insets); exhibits in the Berlinische Galerie and a light installation at the Hamburger Bahnhof (right).

BERLIN'S MODERN ART MUSEUMS

It was not easy to unite the modern art collections of East and West Berlin after reunification, because the national galleries either side of the Wall had forged very different paths. The West had been collecting European and international art; the East had dedicated itself to the art of the GDR. Combining the collections in the Neue Nationalgalerie (new national gallery), which was designed by Ludwig Mies van der Rohe, brought about an "iconoclastic controversy," and a re-assessment of values from both sides. What resulted is a historic divide that extends through the collection of classic modernity right up to the 1970s. The loss of 20th-century works of art, condemned by the National Socialists, has only partially been counterbalanced at this point. Today, however, works by critical realists such as Otto Dix and George Grosz are once again the highlights among the 20th-century paintings and sculptures exhibited on the lower floor. Contemporary art and the Marx collection, comprising works by Joseph Beuys and Andy Warhol, can be seen in the converted Hamburger Bahnhof and at the nearby Sammlung Friedrich Christian Flick. A third exhibit is at the Stüler building with the Berggruen Picasso Collection, while the Berlinische Galerie in Kreuzberg exhibits modern art from Berlin.

As has long been the case, Berlin's western heart beats on Breitscheid-platz, where the damaged tower of the Kaiser-Wilhelm-Gedächtnis-kirche juts admonishingly into the sky next to the shiny blue new church by Eiermann (inset). The site is home to the Kaufhaus des Westens department store, start of the Kurfürstendamm. Schloss Charlottenburg (below) is also in Berlin's western section.

CHARLOTTENBURG, WILMERSDORF

The city's second center, and the manifestation of the wealthy west, includes such icons as Kurfürstendamm, Schloss Charlottenburg, the Zoo and the Olympia Stadium. Up-scale façades fill the side streets, particularly in Charlottenburg, but Wilmersdorf is actually more prosperous. Its widows are still celebrated in the legendary Berlin musical *Linie 1*. After reunification, the historic Mitte district enjoyed more attention as the city's new center, but the tourists have since returned – and the locals never left.

For the city's 750th birthday in 1987, Kurfürstendamm was transformed into an avenue of sculptures. Brigitte and Martin Matschinsky-Denninghoff called their flexible tubes *Berlin* (below); they still accompany the Kaiser-Wilhelm-Gedächtniskirche (church) on Tauentzienstrasse with their swirling shapes. A few steps down towards Wittenbergplatz is the Kaufhaus des Westens, or KaDeWe, a top department store (right) with a legendary delicatessen where gourmets will enjoy choosing among 1,300 cheeses and 2,400 wines from all around the world.

Tauentzien and Breitscheidplatz

The buildings are all less than fifty years old on Tauentzienstrasse, and yet the legendary Golden Twenties seem to live on here. Kurfürstendamm (or Ku'damm) is actually at its liveliest on this street, where the neighborhood hasn't even officially begun. Unfortunately, the nightly air raids of 1943 destroyed a vibrant district that was home to the legendary Romanisches Café as well as some beautiful movie houses. With them went the film stars, poets and musicians. At the time, what is today's old West was then the new West, where exiled Russian poets like Andrei Bely rhapsodized about the "department store of department stores" and the "Night. Tauentzien. Cocaine" atmosphere. The "children from Bahnhof Zoo", characters in a famous book, suffered their heroin addictions here while the beautiful, the Parisian, was just a short ride away to the west.

Next to the ruins of a building from the Wilhelminian era is a flat, grey octagon with a hexagonal tower (below) and a delicately preserved ceiling mosaic (right). Visitors are greeted by a radiant blue (right), created by 33,000 glass bricks manufactured in Chartres, France, but the blue has patches of red, green and yellow light as well, because the architect surrounded the glasshouse with a second octagonal structure with walls 2.5 cm (1 inch) thin. The space in between muffles the noise from the streets and makes room for lamps, which illuminate the cubes.

Kaiser-Wilhelm-Gedächtniskirche

"All things pass" was the theme of the sermon held in the Kaiser-Wilhelm-Gedächtniskirche (memorial church) on November 22, 1943 – "Dead" Sunday. Soon after, the church was in ruins. It has since become known in Berlin as the "hollow tooth": the west belfry was reduced from 113 to 63 m (371 to 207 ft) and totally gutted by bombs. Built in 1895, on orders from Wilhelm II to honor his grandfather and give the new west a monu-ment, the romanesque church was meant to be a draw for the elegant residential and shopping boulevard of Kurfürstendamm as well. Wilhelm also wanted to fight the "rebellious tendencies of an anarchistic and faithless party" (the Social Democrats), and saw its as a unifying symbol for church and monarchy. Despite what is repre-sented, Berliners did not want the ruin torn down. Egon Eiermann built a new church next to it in 1961.

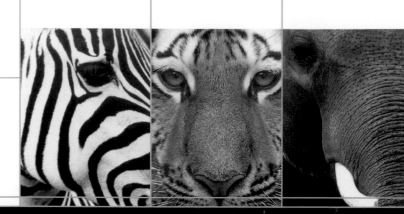

Certainly, the zoological garden in Berlin is worth seeing, if for nothing other than the zebras, the Siberian tiger and the elephants (right). But the zoo's architecture is equally fascinating (below). From the beginning, the animal habitats were built in exotic styles and, although most of the architecture was destroyed during the war, what remained was carefully restored. The parts that were destroyed were rebuilt. As a result, some of the animals live in Arabian mosques or Indian palaces, in North American forts or African clay citadels.

Zoologischer Garten, Aquarium

Berlin has long confused visitors with its Zoo, Tierpark and Tiergarten. To set it straight, there are two zoos, and the Tiergarten (animal garden) is in fact a park. The largest zoo is the Tierpark in Friedrichsfelde in the east, which covers eleven football fields. But the most famous zoo, whose visitor numbers are only surpassed by the Reichstag dome, is the Zoologischer Garten. It covers only 32 hectares (79 acres), but boasts the greatest num-

ber of animal species in Europe. Germany's first zoo, it was opened in 1844, on the initiative of Alexander von Humboldt and landscape architect Peter Joseph Lenné, and stocked with Friedrich Wilhelm IV's menagerie, previously based on the Pfaueninsel (peacock island). Zoologist Alfred Brehm founded the aquarium, which has over 10,000 creatures. Berliners love their animals, and all births and deaths are public events.

The works of Berlin artist Cornelia Schleime (below, left and center) have been shown in Amsterdam and Buffalo. Dutch artist Bas Meermann (right) works in Berlin, as do (right) Norbert Bisky, J-Bo Monkey, art director of the magazine *Style*, and Eberhard Havekost.

YOUNG ART

It started with the galleries that were set up after the fall of the Wall in the Mitte district, when the plaster was crumbling from the walls and ceilings, and the floorboards were rotten under foot. At the time, spaces had been rented cheaply to starving artists before speculators knew their efforts would pay off. Now, what was once a handful of galleries in the east has become hundreds. Kunst-Werke (art works), for example, opened in a decaying old margarine factory. Today it is known as the KW Institute for Contemporary Art, one of Germany's most important centers for contemporary art, and internationally renowned. Young artists from around the world have presented their work in their first solo exhibitions here, and the Berlin Biennial for Contemporary Art was founded here in 1997. Every year, the Messe Art Forum attracts increasing numbers of international art lovers to Berlin. Once dominated by painting, art has now evolved to include conceptual trends as well as methods for working with space and installations. Since 1997, the Berlin Art Autumn has showcased contemporary visual arts and in 2006, a jubilee exhibition showed the work of sixty artists from twenty-one nations who lived and worked in Berlin. It seems to have just scratched the surface of a vibrantly growing scene.

Shopping is exhausting, but you can always recover in the street cafés, and, like in Paris, people often sit next to each other facing the street in order to see and be seen (below). The old Kranzler Café (right) has had trouble keeping up with the more popular street cafés with its new design. The high-end shoppers (far right), who worry very little about the prices on the menu or on the labels, have migrated to the upper Ku'damm, near Olivaer Platz. The small, vibrant boutiques and their playful decorations are now hidden away in the side streets.

Kurfürstendamm

The original plan was to give the imperial capital a boulevard modelled on the Champs-Elysées in Paris. Chancellor Otto von Bismarck suggested it after returning from Paris at the end of the Franco-Prussian War. As a result, the former road between Berlin's west and the Grunewald hunting lodge was transformed into a 3.5-km-long (2-mile), 53-m-wide (174-ft) grand avenue, and anyone who could afford it moved in right away.

People here are happy to ignore the hulking or the neoclassical, the playful or the gaudy. All eyes are glued to the window displays, checking goods and prices. And the stores change with the fashions in order to compete with the still very new Old Mitte district, which deprives them of the tourists, but not the hordes of shoppers. Kurfürstendamm has remained Berlin's number one, at least as a shopping street.

Bertolt Brecht's *Mother Courage* doesn't just pull her cart across the Berliner Ensemble stage (below). In 2006, the Admiralspalast was reopened with this Brecht play. Far right: The highwaymen's running wheel matches the offbeat reputation of Castorfs Volksbühne (folk theater). The Schaubühne am Lehniner Platz glitters with Sasha Waltz's choreography, and at the Maxim Gorki Theater, Katharina Thalbach regularly graces the stage. The odd one out is the Friedrichstadtpalast, which has been staging revues since GDR times (right).

BERLIN'S THEATERS

Nobody knows for certain, but there must be a hundred or more. Many of them pop up suddenly before disappearing without a trace again. A venue is created, and the next day it is gone, just like the ruins of the Palast der Republik when it was stripped of asbestos. Indeed, a vital part of German theater history was and still is being written in Berlin. Gerhart Hauptmann, August Strindberg, Henrik Ibsen and Bertolt Brecht all had their breakthroughs here. Directors such as Max Reinhardt, Erwin Piscator and Gustaf Gründgens remain unforgettable, and Peter Stein and his projects are still showstoppers today. German classics, classical modern drama, contemporary American, British, Russian and French plays, experimental, criminal and dance theater, they all have their place here alongside comedies and people's theater. Theater rendezvous and visiting troupes provide new impulses as well. It almost goes without saying that such a full repertoire also includes special performances for children. The most famous of all Berlin's children's stages, the Grips Theater became a local legend with its version of *Line 1* – still the play with the highest number of performances in German-speaking countries. The Schaubude meanwhile, a puppet theater, is much more than just another Punch and Judy show.

Industrial landmarks: the gasometer and the water tower (below), and the radio tower (far right). Right: The Hoffmann kiln hall at the porcelain factory can be rented, while the Wuhlheide water works still use their space themselves. Classic cars are on display at the former tram depot.

INDUSTRIAL MONUMENTS

Cold stores and warehouses, hangars for horse-drawn vehicles, waterworks, steam mills and gas works. All relics of another time. Entire factory towns sprang up during industrialization, which marked Berlin's development starting in the 19th century and eventually turned it into the largest manufacturing city in Europe. Industry has largely disappeared now, but many of its remnants are still part of the cityscape today, even if it is no longer clear what they once were. At the time, new production methods put new demands on architecture, but the aesthetic development of industrial buildings also influenced its clients: grand façades were created in diverse styles, from Neoclassicism to Art Nouveau. The turbine hall, commissioned in 1908 for the production of steam turbines by AEG founder, Emil Rathenau, is considered the starting point of modern industrial architecture in Germany. Technological progress was not hidden in this massive temple of glass, steel and concrete, but rather put on display. Today, the towers of the Borsig company contain a shopping mall, for example; horse stables have been transformed into a cinema; singers perform in bus depots; and designers work in electricity substations. The electricity works are now a dance club, and plays are performed at a brewery. People even live in an old water tower.

Spectators are protected not by a roof but by an open ring of Teflon-coated fiberglass (below) and there is plenty of high-tech entertainment as well (inset bottom).Right: International track & field events take place here as well as Hertha BSC games, Berlin's top soccer team.

Olympia Stadium

The foundations are old. The canopy is new, and carefully added on to merge past and present. It is the site of the 1936 Olympic Games, when the entire world still believed that Hitler's Germany was a tolerant state. It is also where the final of the 2006 World Cup was played, and a venue for track & field events including the World Championships in 2009. The crisp design is based on ancient sports arenas and since steel construction was not sufficiently grand when it was originally built, natural flagstone slabs provided the desired gravitas. Neither architects nor the building's heritage status were able to prevent the blue track – blue stands for Hertha BSC, Berlin's top soccer club. On the oval's western side, the marathon gate provides views of the Maifeld, where dressage and polo contests take place, as well as of the belfry and the Waldbühne.

Two warriors defend the entrance to Schloss Charlottenburg, with its equestrian statue of the Great Elector Friedrich Wilhelm (below). Inset: A statue of Prince Albrecht of Prussia in Schlossstrasse. Right: Life-sized sculptures represent the muses.

Charlottenburg Palace

The most important historical edifice in the western part of Berlin, built in 1699 by Johann Arnold Nering, and at the time named Lietzenburg, only received its present name after the death of Queen Sophie Charlotte, its first chatelaine. In 1701, when Elector Friedrich III crowned himself King Friedrich I of Prussia in Königsberg, the baroque central portion of the summer palace was no longer sufficient. The palace was enlarged in 1713 to include the Orangery and the Kuppelturm before Friedrich the Great had a new wing constructed. By the time Friedrich Wilhelm III had added the palace theater in 1791, the palace already measured 505 m (1,657 ft). Charlottenburg was almost completely destroyed in 1943, but today, after years of restoration, it has been restored to its former glory. Locals now stroll among French and English garden scenery.

The Türkenmarkt at Kottbusser Tor in the Kreuzberg district is a local institution. One of Germany's largest Turkish communities lives here, in one of Berlin's poorest but most vibrant districts (inset).

Since the fall of the Wall, Prenzlauer Berg (below) has transformed itself from a working-class district into a trendy area for young, educated people from all over the East and West.

PRENZLAUER BERG, FRIEDRICHSHAIN, KREUZBERG, TEMPELHOF

This sprawling city – covering 892 sq km (344 sq miles) – is continuously evolving. As late as 1920, eight towns, fifty-nine rural communes and twenty-seven country estates were incorporated into Greater Berlin, which made the city's population swell to nearly four million. After a merger in 2001, twenty-three districts were merged into twelve, and they fight hard to preserve their identities. Berliners are very loyal to their *kiez* (quarter), whether it's Prenzlauer Berg, Friedrichshain, Kreuzberg or Tempelhof.

Plenty of space for culture at the old brewery (below), for example, for the RambaZamba theater (right), whose plays are coproduced by disabled people; for disabled painters; for air guitar championships; and for for rocking fans (insets bottom).

KulturBrauerei

Above the doors are signs for the hayloft, bottled beer, stables, saddlers and cartwrights; it all once formed an entire brewery complex. The brick fortress on the block between Schönhauser Allee and Knaackstrasse was built around the turn of the 20th century and housed the Schultheiss brewery until 1965. Then East Berlin rockers in leather stormed the old canteen and, after the fall of the Wall, the heritage site quickly became famous as the KulturBrauerei (culture brewery). Everyone wanted a space in the venerable but run-down venue, which suited alternative lifestyles perfectly. It was then renovated and became increasingly attractive, almost too attractive. Cinemas and beer houses moved in; workshops and studios out. Now, it all coexists here, from reading stages and dance events to the Sonnenuhr (sundial), a workshop that integrates disabled people.

All of Berlin's synagogues are open for services. Right: Patterns incorporating the Star of David in Germany's largest Synagogue in Rykestrasse, and window designs in other places of worship. Insets below: Festive garb, a religious service, a visit by the chief rabbi and a store selling kosher goods. Large pictures, from left: A glimpse of the interior of two synagogues. The cloaked torah scrolls at the Rykestrasse Synagogue contain the sacred five books of Moses, written on parchment.

JEWISH LIFE

In 1933, about 160,000 Jews were living in Berlin. In 1939, half of them had already left the country. Roughly 55,000 were then deported, locked into cattle cars at the Grunewald S-Bahn station, transported to extermination camps and murdered. In 1945, many of the 8,000 survivors waited in vast emigration halls for their visas to leave the country. Meanwhile, Berlin's oldest Jewish cemetery in Grosse Hamburger Strasse had been destroyed and the largest Jewish cemetery in Europe, in the Weissensee district, is still in need of urgent restoration. Today, the Jewish community here again numbers 12,000 members, but the capital suffers from the loss of an elite, which historically dictated cultural life not just of the city but of an entire epoch; it had included painters like Max Liebermann and Lesser Ury; philosophers such as Martin Buber and Ludwig Marcuse; physicist Albert Einstein; writers Kurt Tucholsky, Lion Feuchtwanger and Walter Benjamin; publishers Samuel Fischer, Rudolf Mosse and Leopold Ullstein. The list seems endless. But the number of Jewish institutions in Berlin is growing again. The Central Council of Jews in Germany reassumed its work in Berlin in 1999, Jewish theaters have been established, people visit their synagogues, and museums tell of everyday life in Berlin before the war.

Multicultural life in the city is at its best than during the Carnival of Cultures. The samba dancer and her plumage (below) is part of it, as are the those with red clown noses, happy artists, and an increasing number of spectators in their own fantasy costumes (right).

CARNIVAL OF CULTURES

The Caribbean and various other countries come alive in Kreuzberg at Whitsun (Pentecost). The Carnival here was started by the Werkstatt der Kulturen (Workshop of Cultures) in 1996, to promote the cultural potential of Berlin's immigrants and allow others to experience these cultures. Over the years, it has blossomed into a street festival that is now enjoyed by millions of visitors. The carnival procession has nearly 1,000 artist participants and snakes along Hasenheide in Kreuzberg for the entire day. There are people with masks, live music, decorated floats and dancers – spectators are moved by the infectious rhythms. Some 450,000 foreigners live in Berlin, and even those who do not celebrate carnival at home still showcase their own cultures with masks, costumes and local music in order to make their participation in the local patchwork visible. People of all ages participate in the festival including many immigrant associations as well as local youth and cultural institutions. The preparations for the next festival actually begin as soon as the current one finishes. Materials have to be acquired for the elaborate costumes, which then have to be sewn; the choreography has to be organized; and the music has to be selected and studied – all so that next year's festival will be even better.

The two tower blocks on Straus-berger Platz (below) open out to a 90-m-wide (98-yd) street – ideal, and often used, for processions and parades. The façades of the houses were originally decorated with ceramic tiles (right), until the Meissen workshops could no longer satisfy the demand. The tiles even-tually began falling off, so locals mocked the street as "Rue de Duo-san" (after an all-purpose glue).

Karl-Marx-Allee

On September 21, 1949, this street, no more than a rubble heap, was named Stalinallee on the occasion of the Soviet dictator's 70th birthday. The name was meant to be a legacy, and the boulevard grand. However, it was more often vilified as a cookie-cutter Soviet advertisement and is now nothing more than a remnant of the Cold War. Of course, it was supposed to demonstrate the superiority of socialism over capitalism, but town planners also wrestled with the cityscape's significance and style. To the sound of work songs, rubble was cleaned up and stones were moved to make room for housing. The artificial pathos of the residential buildings eventually failed, however, due to the DDR's overestimation of its own economic strength. The workers' rebellion of June 17, 1953, began here. The 2.3-km (1.5-mile) street has long since become a heritage site.

In the autumn of 1990, 110 artists from twenty-four countries turned the Wall on the eastern banks of the Spree into an open-air gallery (right). Every November 9, candles burn at the Mauergedenkstätte in Bernauer Strasse to commemorate the fall of the Wall (below).

THE WALL

During the night of August 13, 1961, GDR border troops began building the "anti-fascist protective barrier" designed to prevent the flight of people from East Berlin to West Berlin. For twenty-eight years, the Wall separated families and represented a global division. After the fall of the Wall, in a state of euphoria, people knocked off, tore down, divided up, sold, gave away and, finally, shredded for the construction of roads everything that reminded them of that division. Ultimately, both visitors and Berliners were no longer sure where exactly the Wall had once stood. Today, a cycle track retraces the Wall's former course for 155 km (93 miles) through and around the city, and a paved strip in the asphalt marks its path. It was not until 2006 that people felt the need to erect a memorial, and the city council assisted in doing so. The feeling of everyday violence that was once linked with the Wall is now lost. It lives on in the memory of individuals but is hard to convey to outsiders. It is very difficult to imagine a wall cutting across the city, permanently lit, with 293 watchtowers, dog runs, patrol paths, spring-loaded guns, anti-tank barricades and a 100-m-wide (109-yd) noman's land. Two hundred and thirty-seven "escapees from the republic" were killed by firearms and thirty-three by mines.

Views of the Spree: The new embankment promenade between Reichstag and Hauptbahnhof (below); the Trias building next to the Michaelbrücke (right); the Reichstag and the Federal Ministry of the Interior in Moabit (insets, from left).

ALONG THE SPREE

They say Berlin was built from a barge. In fact, the Spree, which originates beneath the peak of 583-m-high (1,913-ft) Kottmar Mountain in Upper Lusatia, has always mainly been a transport route. Even the recent building sites at Potsdamer Platz and the new central station were supplied with building materials transported along the Spree. Standing on the Weidendamm bridge in Mitte, you will often see barges and passenger ships. A boat trip is actually one of the most entertaining ways to explore Berlin. Slowly and quietly, you glide through the city, which has more waterways than any other European metropolis: There are 180 km (112 miles) of navigable river including the Spree, Havel and other canals. Some people live in their boats on the Spree, although officially houseboats do not exist. You can see them in parts of Charlottenburg now, where the washing flutters in the wind on the Spree at Treptow. Many industrial structures line the Spree as well, but now that the first developers and embassies have discovered these attractive locations, residential buildings are springing up on the banks and architects create demand for "floating homes." Restaurant boats bob in the water, and at last it is possible again to swim in the Spree, even if only in the Badeschiff, a barge that has been converted into a swimming pool.

The Martin-Gropius-Bau is resplendent with columns and prestigious exhibitions (right). The Deutsches Technikmuseum hosts the Z 5, for example, one of the first computers (inset, below), a steam-driven tugboat (facing page) and the interior of the Jean Cousin (left).

Martin-Gropius-Bau, Deutsches Technikmuseum

Two of Berlin's most attractive museums, from among roughly 170 in total, are located in Kreuzberg. The Kunstgewerbemuseum (applied arts), built in a neo-Renaissance style in 1881 by Martin Gropius, was intended to inspire Prussian artisans with beautiful works from around the world. The façade relief features blacksmiths, basketmakers and glassblowers. After its renovation, the museum has consistently put on spectacular shows in its atrium. The Deutsches Technikmuseum (technology museum), founded in just 1982 to house various existing collections, is a fascinating journey through the cultural history of technology, from the world's first computer and the development of automation in industry, to the technologies of navigation, aviation and communication. It exhibits locomotives, classic cars, an old brewery and the interactive Science Center spectrum.

Symbols of Jewish history (right): the Holocaust Tower, the Garden of Emigrants, and shafts that admit daylight from outside into the interior. On the far right are old images and a Hebrew writing installation, which is meant to puzzle visitors initially.

Jewish Museum

A broken Star of David: an architectural quirk or just a shiny metallic zigzag? Long before it opened, it was already creating a stir. The zinc coating of the building reflects sunlight, slits and wedges seem to be scribbled onto windowless walls, and there is no entrance. Visitors enter the building, designed by Daniel Libeskind, via the baroque Supreme Court building and find themselves in a historically coded aesthetic space. Empty rooms, which the architect calls "voids," extend across all floors, symbolizing a lost culture. Only the narrow slits admit light into the building, promising hope. Darkness and emptiness characterize the Holocaust Tower. The garden, where olive branches grow in concrete columns, is a symbol for the fate of emigrants. Two thousand years of German-Jewish history, from Roman times to the present day, are displayed here.

Old traditions seem to disappear, but that is because Kreuzberg tolerates different lifestyles. Everyone shops in the Turkish market at Maybachufer (below), while many of the Turkish institutions, such as travel agents (far right), are used only by the Turkish community. Headscarves and long coats are not the rule. Many young women have long been wearing Western style clothes (inset, top right). Most of those holding prayer beads or visiting the mosque are fathers and grandfathers (right).

TURKISH KREUZBERG

The largest Turkish community outside of Turkey – some 200,000 people – has its main hub around the Kottbusser Tor in Kreuzberg. Turkish jewellers, banks, grocers, clothing stores, bakers and coffee houses create an exotic ambience along with the market at Maybachufer. Twice a week, this market causes traffic chaos in the streets around it, because many families buy their food staples in bulk here, or perhaps curtains and cutlery. There is a Turkish radio station and a TV channel, and an agency specializes in booking belly dancers. During the Cold War, when cheap and affordable housing was still available, so called "guest workers" settled here, in the shadow of the Wall. They were not planning to stay for the long term, but between 1960 and 1970 their numbers had already risen from 225 to 39,000. At the same time, SO 36, the northern district of Kreuzberg, named after the imperial postal district, became a destination for all those who wished to escape "Prussian" narrow-mindedness. It developed into a multicultural experiment. Today, women of all nationalities meet at the Turkish hammam (bath house), a deli sells Arab finger food and above the Rote Harfe (red harp), the legendary meeting point for Kreuzberg "revolutionaries", the in-crowd puffs on a water pipe in the Orient Lounge.

The arrivals hall was often used as a film set (picture series below). Tempelhof's real-life history began in the 1920s. The 1948/49 Berlin Blockade was a legend – every child knew the term "raisin bomber" (picture series above and full picture).

TEMPELHOF

Some people were overcome by melancholy and others sensed relief when Tempelhof closed on 30 October 2008. This small, centrally located airport was an obstacle to plans for a major Berlin airport. For a long time, Tempelhof was unable to meet the demands of modern travel, being more of a museum than state-of-the-art hub.

Scheduled flights operated only between Friedrichshafen or Mannheim. But Tempelhof had seen better days. Beginning in 1923 under Adolf Hitler, the airport terminal's massive architecture was to become part of a future imperial capital of "Germania". Yet Tempelhof will live on people's memories because of the allied airlift:

in late June 1948, after the Soviet Union blocked access routes to West Berlin during the Berlin Blockade, allied pilots flew missions supplying Berlin with food. The renamed "raisin bombers" became legendary until September 1949, as supplies of powdered milk and chocolate and also coal and industrial goods were trans-

ported via the air corridor. There is still no consensus about Tempelhof's future. In 2009, the fashion fair "Bread & Butter" secured usage rights for the next decade. Other ideas are for a cultural centre, residential districts or parkland – the site of the former airfield covers more than two square kilometres.

Jonathan Borofsky's three Molecule Men out in the Spree symbolize the districts of Kreuzberg, Friedrichshain and Treptow, which meet roughly at this point (below). The embankment has an urban face, yet hidden in its tributary canals are floating restaurants, and Treptower Park and Plänterwald park are also nearby. Far from the center is the Müggelsee, in the district of Köpenick (inset).

BEYOND THE CITY CENTERS

Many Berliners live in green areas that are not always far from the city center. Berlin is not the concrete jungle you might think it is. If you include water and open spaces, roughly 40 percent of the city's area is undeveloped. Even in the center, large and small pockets of green pop up everywhere. The outlying forests, rivers and lakes are popular daytrip destinations as well. During the days of the Wall, West Berliners had no alternative if they did not wish to suffer the lengthy waiting periods at the checkpoints.

The city once ended at the Ober-baumbrücke (below) between Kreuz-berg and Friedrichshain where, at night, a floating tree barricade blocked the entrance. Today, swimmers can venture out until midnight to the Badeschiff (right) and enjoy nights on the "beach".

Treptow, Friedrichsfelde

The district of Treptow, although close to the inner city, has large recreation spaces such as Plänterwald and Treptower Park. The park alongside the Spree was created during the days of industrialization, to "lift the spirit and moderate negative attitudes". Now, on the banks of the Spree, industrial relics from that time await a new purpose. Some idyllic conversions have taken place too: the Arena cultural center, the Badeschiff (swimming barge) and a boat restaurant. A hydroplane takes off here for sightseeing trips, and in the port, scheduled boats leave for Spree cruises. The main attraction in Friedrichsfelde is the Tierpark. Built on the palace grounds in 1954, the zoo covers 160 hectares (395 acres). On 23 km (14 miles) of paths, visitors are led past ponds and trenches, lion and crocodile enclosures, monkey islands and buffalo and bison pastures.

A permanent exhibition in Köpenick town hall (right) documents the story of how an ex-convict snubbed the authorities; a bronze "Hauptmann" stands outside (below). Famous captains include Otto Sander (far right), Heinz Rühmann, Harald Juhnke and Katharina Thalbach.

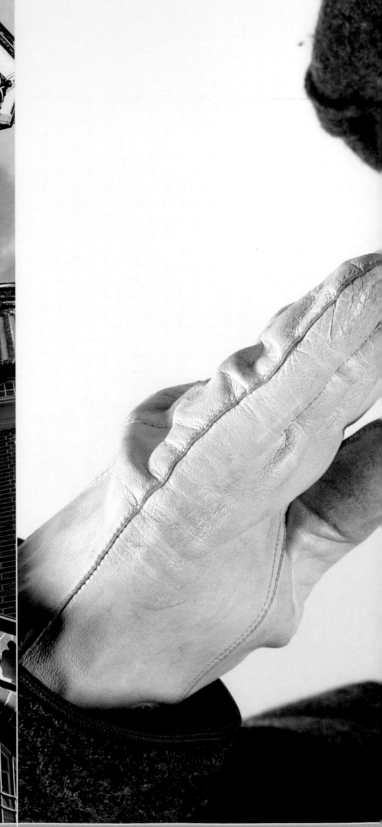

"THE CAPTAIN OF KÖPENICK"

In 1906, the 57-year-old shoemaker Wilhelm Voigt from Tilsit made Köpenick famous, the home of Berlin's largest woods and most extensive waterways. On Voigt's release after a prison sentence, the authorities prevented his return to civilian life – he could not find work in Potsdam and had been expelled from Berlin. Frustrated, he went to second-hand dealers and bought all the items that would identify him as a captain of the First Guards Regiment. He then took twelve grenadiers from the military baths at Plötzensee under his command, travelled with his troop by train to Köpenick, and arrested first the treasurer and then the mayor, Dr. Langerhans. A carriage was ordered to take the mayor and his wife to the Neue Wache in Berlin, where they would be informed of the reasons for their arrest. Voigt himself, together with two of his soldiers, then entered the council treasury. He declared control of the local administration and began checking the accounts. He demanded that two bags be brought so he could carry away the 4,002 Marks that he found, and announced that he had confiscated the money. He ordered his troop to return and travelled to Berlin by himself. A tip-off from a former fellow inmate led to Voigt's arrest. Carl Zuckmayer turned the impostor into a literary character.

Called the "Bridge of Unity" by the GDR, it later became famous as the "Bridge of Spies". Today it is again the Glienicker Brücke (right). Fabled creatures line the griffon gate, which leads into the Glienicker Schloss (insets). Below: Banisters of the "Grosse Neugierde" viewing pavilion.

Glienicker Schloss, Glienicker Brücke

Part of the cultural complex of Potsdam is located in Berlin's far south-west corner where, from 1600, the ruling Hohenzollerns commissioned famous architects and horticulturalists, such as Schinkel, Persius and Lenné, to create a paradise landscape of parks, palaces and villas on important stretches of the Havel river. Prince Carl acquired Klein-Glienicke in 1824, commissioning Schinkel with the palace conversion and Lenné and Baron von Pückler-Muskau with the garden design. A "leisure garden" was created around the palace that stretched down to the river banks. Karl Friedrich Schinkel also designed the Glienicker Brücke, on the site of both an earlier wooden bridge dating from 1663 and a drawbridge. In 1907, it was replaced by an iron bridge that became famous as the "Bridge of Spies", where East and West exchanged secret agents during the Cold War.

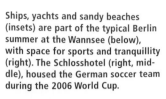

Ships, yachts and sandy beaches (insets) are part of the typical Berlin summer at the Wannsee (below), with space for sports and tranquillity (right). The Schlosshotel (right, middle), housed the German soccer team during the 2006 World Cup.

Grunewald, Wannsee

Today, like a hundred years ago, the Grunewald forest and villa colony is the most exclusive area in Berlin. Established on the initiative of Bismarck, the nameless doorbells hint at well-known residents. The well-heeled have also set up colonies of country mansions in the Zehlendorf districts of Schlachtensee and Wannsee. Politicians, opera singers, industrialists, publishers, poets and composers all appreciate the green surroundings. It was from S-Bahn station Grunewald, built in the style of an English country house, that Berlin's Jews were taken away to extermination camps, among them local residents. The new landlords then moved into the beautiful houses. Today, Grunewald is still a popular daytrip destination for Berliners. It has many attractive swimming lakes, including Grosser and Kleiner Wannsee, which were originally large coves in the Havel river.

In this small 18th-century palace (right), designed by the architect Johann Brendel to look like a fortress (a fashion at the time), visitors can admire the unique original furnishings comprising diversely patterned parquet floors, fabric wallpaper, armchairs with horsehair upholstery and imaginative details such as swivel chairs. Sightlines reveal views of other buildings as well. You will hear the plaintive cry of the approximately thirty-five peacocks, and if you are lucky you may see the stunning display of their iridescent plumage (below).

ATLAS

The cradle of Berlin lies on an island in the Spree river, in the heart of the city. It was here, as early as 1443, that the foundation stone for the city palace was laid. To this day, numerous historic sites lie between the Spree island and the Brandenburg Gate. The area to the east of the Spree island has been redeveloped with modern buildings. Since reunification, Spandauer Vorstadt, a district north of the Spree, has become popular for a night out. In the historic center, Friedrichstrasse and the Gendarmenmarkt are good for a stroll.

Berlin boasts a very dense local transport network. The S-Bahn also stops at the splendid new Hauptbahnhof (central station), which was put into operation in May 2006.

MAP LEGEND
1 : 20 000

	Motorway (expressway)
	Important major road (under construction)
	Main road
	Other road
	Footpath
	Pedestrian zone
	Railway (railroad)
	Industrial railway (railroad)
	S-Bahn line (suburban trains)
	Underground line (under construction / planned)
	Car ferry; important passenger ferry
	Densely built-up area; thinly built-up area
	Public buildings
	Important building; industrial building
	Green spaces; cemetery; forest
	Jewish cemetery

170-171   172-173
168-169
174-175   176-177

LEGEND

The maps on the following pages represent the city of Berlin at a scale of 1:20,000. The cartographic details are supplemented by a multitude of useful tips for tourists, indicating the public transport network, which is shown in detail, as well as icons marking location and type of important sights, such as museums, palaces, government offices or theaters.

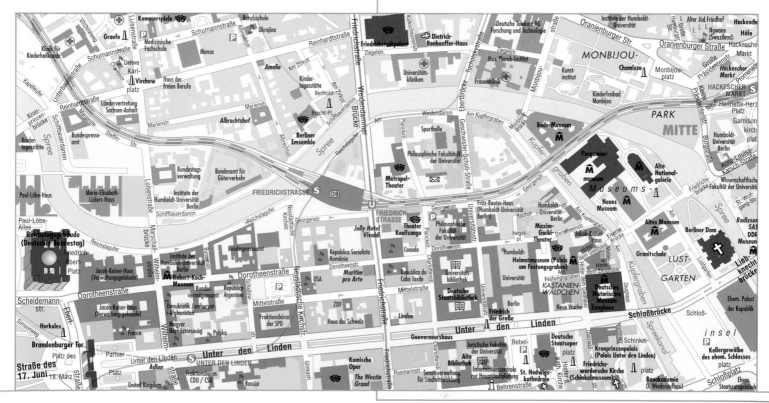

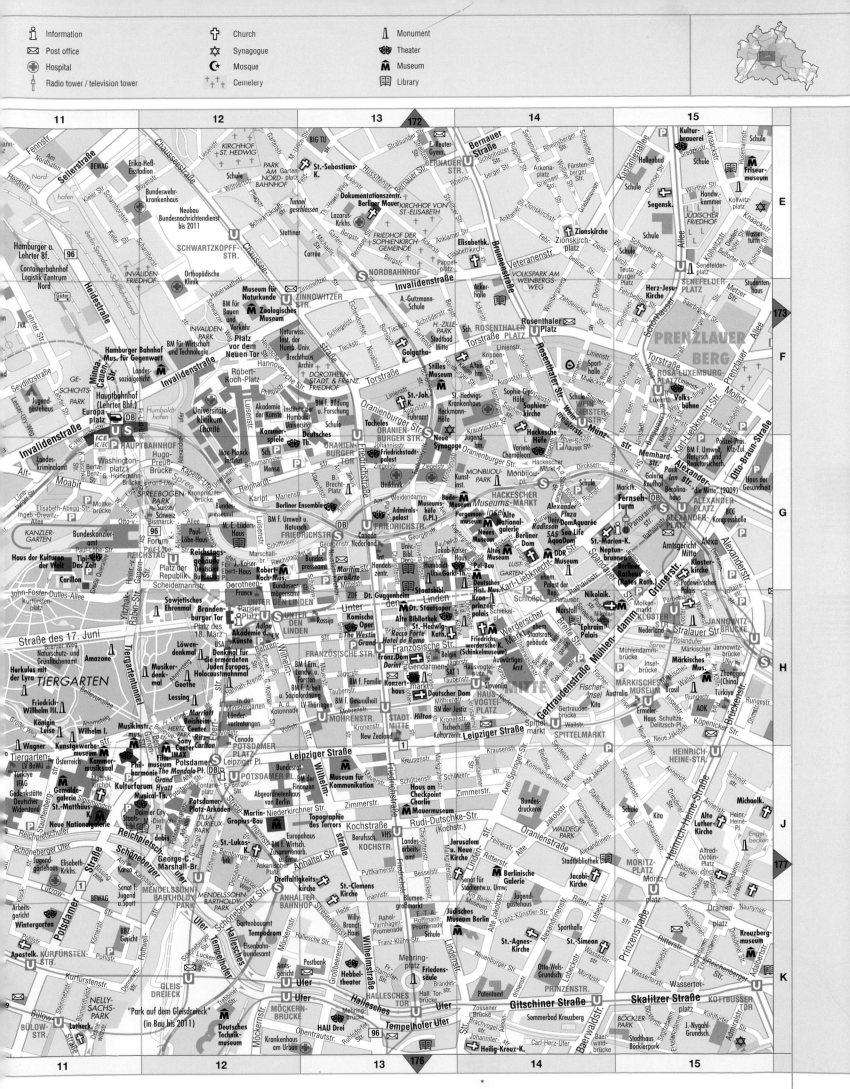

100 Motorway number
1 Federal road number
15 Motorway exit number
One-way street

Airport
Central station
ICE IC/EC Station for express trains
DB Station for intercity railway transportation

S S-Bahn station
U U-Bahn station
Bus terminal
P+R Park + Ride

P P Car park
Stadium
Trade fair
Embassy

Flughafen Berlin-Tegel „Otto Lilienthal"
(schließt 2011 kurz nach der Eröffnung des neuen Flughaf

Terminal Empfangsgebäude
Tower

Jungfern-heide

Rev. Försterei Tegel Süd
Malchwerweg
Kolonie Am Tegeler See
Kolonie Saatwinkel
Sickerbecken
Kol. Am Hohenzollernkanal
Kolonie Rohrbruchwiesen
Hohenzollernkanal
Bootshausweg
Grützmachergraben
SIEMENSSIEDLG. AM HOHENZOLLERN-KANAL IV
Bernauer Str.
Tegeler Br.
Str. R
Str. S
Str. T
Str. C
Str. L
Str. M
Str. K
Str. J
Str. H
Str. G
Str. F
SIEMENSSIEDLG. AM HOHENZOLLERN-KANAL III
Siemenswerke
GARTEN-FELD
Kolonie am Hohenzollernkanal
Weihnachts-kirche
Saatwinkler
Damm
Gartenfelder Str.
P
HASEL-
HORST
Adlerweg
Lerchenweg
Finkenmasse
Nachtigallweg
Steglitz-weg
Schulweg
Feld IV
Kolonie Vor den Toren
Feld III
Weg 5
Weg 4
Weg 3
Weg 2
Weg 1
Sing-
Mäckeritz-wiesen
Kolonie Beussel'sche Erben
Kolonie Neuland II
Mecklenburgweg
Brandenburgweg
Apfelweg
Kirschenweg
Kolonie Neuland I
Kolonie Köppen'sche Erben
Kolonie Fabian'sche Erben
Kol. Am Wasserbunker
Hohlweg
Kol. Am Mäckeritzweg
Str. A
Str. B
Kolonie Vor den Toren Feld II
Ostpreußenweg
Kolonie Vor den Toren Feld I
Veitlinweg
Nelkenweg
Hauptweg
Rosenweg
Dahlienweg
Hohlweg
Zollamt
Hohenzollernkanal
Saatwinkler Damm
Alter Berlin-Spandauer Schifffahrtskanal
Senioren-wohnheim
Kolonie Am Rohrdamm
Ruderleistungs-zentrum
Sportplätze Jungfernheide
Baumschule
VOLKSPARK
Saatwinkler
Weg
Kanalstr.
der Weg
Burschorster Damm
Senioren-Freizeitstätte
Gartenfelder Straße
Sch.
Kita
St.-Stephanus
Senioren-wohnhaus
Großmarkt
Knobelsdorff-Oberschule
OSZ Bau- und Holztechnik
P
Kolonie Gartenfreunde Siemensstadt
Neuap. Kirche
Haselhorster Weg
Kolonie Siemens-stadt
Kolonie Neuer Exerzierplatz
Sport- und Freizeitzentrum Siemensstadt
Sporthalle
Buolstr.
Kolonie Alter Exerzierplatz
Paulsternstr.
außer Betrieb
Rohrdamm
Harriesstr.
Rapsstr.
Rieppelstr.
Köttgenstr.
Janisstr.
Dihlmannstr.
Bingel-str.
Im Heide-winkel
Eichengrund
Am Laubwald
Jungfernheideweg
Kolonie Am Rohrdamm
C.-Fr.-v.-Siemens-OS
J. G. Halske-OS
WILHELM-VON-SIEMENS-PARK
Rodel-bahn
Schuckert-platz
Schuckert-str.
Jungfern-heideteich
Freibad Jungfernheide
Gustav-Böß-Freilichtbühne Naturtheater
Heckerdamm
Kindererholungs-stätten
Wasserturm
Hinckeldey-denkmal
JUNGFERNHEIDE
SIEMENS-STADT
H.-Hertz-OS
H. Lenthe-weg
Schweiger-steig
Natalisstr.
Goebelstr.
-damm
H.-Löns-Gsch.
Geißlerpfad
Geißlersteig
Schwen-nerweg
Goebel-platz
Toeplerstr.
M.-Bürger-Krkhs.
Heinickew.
H.-J.-von-Moltke-GS
Bürgeramt
Paelchau-OS
Habermann-zeile
Heckerdamm
Nonnendammallee
PAULSTERNSTR.
U
R.-Reinick-GS
Jugend-gstg.
Kapellen-stg.
Halske-steig
Jugend-weg
Jugend-pl.
Mäckeritzstr.
Goebelstr.
Schleppen-horstw.
Letter-hausw.
A.-Freud-OS
Sühne-Christi-K.
HALEMWEG
Nonnendammallee
U
ROHRDAMM
Rohrdamm
Weh-Quellw.
Grammé-str.
Böttcherstr.
Wernerwerkdamm
Wehr-nerstelsig
Hertwegsteig
Ohmstr.
SIEMENSDAMM
Popitzweg
Hellmannring
Hellmannring
P+R
U
Siemens-
damm
JAKOB-KAISER-
Jakob-Kaiser-Pl.
Siemensdamm
13
Unterspree (Alte Spree)
Großer Spreering
Motardstr.
Motardstr.
Sternfelder Str.
Wasserwerk Jungfernheide
Klärbecken
Siemenswerke
Siemens-
damm
N.-Groß-Weg
Nonnen-
Haupt-feuerwehr
5
4 13
AB-Dreieck Charlottenburg
Tegeler
damm
Ottembucht
Kraftwerk Reuter
Kraft-werk
Kolonie Spreewiesen
WILHELM-VON-SIEMENS-PARK
Sickerbecken
Faule Spree
Rohr-dammbr.
Rudolf-Wissell-Br.
Charlottenburger Schleuse
Kolonie Schleusenland
Abfall-beseitigungs-werk Nord
Werkring
Sophienwerderweg
Kolonie Kraftwerk Unterspree
Wiesen-
Faule Spree
Spree
Kolonie Spreewiesen
Fürsten-
brunner Weg
Strichkanal
Spree
Belvedere/KPM-Porzellansamml.
SCHLOSS-
Kolonie Ruhleben
Charlottenburger Chaussee
RUHLEBEN
Wiesen-dammbr.
Kol. Eichtal
Kol. Spreeblick
Kol. Freiland
Kolonie Fürstenbrunn
Kol. Ruhwald
Spreegrund
Kolonie Tiefer Grund
Kolonie Eisenbh.-Landw.
Kolonie Westend
Güterbahnhof Charlottenburg
Güter
Spandauer Damm
Kinderklinik Kaiserin Auguste-Viktoria
Karp-fen-teich
GARTEN
An der Fließweg
Sternweg
Jasminweg
DRK
Machandel-
Rominter Allee
Waldstern
Murellenteich
Kita
PARK RUHWALD
Spreetal-
Spandauer Bock
Kol. Wochen-end
Kol. Spandauer Bock
Kol. Ruhwald
Kolonie Golfplatz Westend
Sportplätze Westend
KAISER-WILHELM-
GED.-KIRCHHOF
Kolonie Fürstenbrunner Weg
Spandauer Damm
Max-Bürger-Krankenhaus
ESCP/EAP
Schlossklinik KG
Schloss-
Senioren-heim Ernst-Bumm-Weg
Mausoleum
Schl Charlott
Museum für Vor- und Frühgeschichte
Mus
Spandauer Damm
Spandauer Bock
Reichsstraße
Gothaallee
Westendallee
Kolonie Westend Braunsfelde Sonntagsfrieden Wasserturm Gesundheitspflege Bismarksruh Rosstrappe Birkenwäldchen
Heinrich-Zille-Weg
Waldschulallee
LUISEN-KIRCHHOF III
Kol. Fürstenbrunner Weg
Institut für Tropenmedizin
DRK-Kliniken Westend
Kinderklinik
Spandauer-Damm-Br.
Spandauer Damm
Gesundheitshaus
Max-Berg
Schl.
Bröhan-museum
Mus
Sportforum
Prinz-Friedrich-Karl-Weg
Jahn-
Haus d. dt. Sports
Adler-pl.
Glockenturmburgpl.
Hinden-
A.-Bier-Platz
Friedrich-Friesen-
Körner-pl.
U-Bahn Haupt- und Betriebswerkstatt Grunewald
U-Bahn-Museum
M
Rossitter Platz
Tennis-stadion
Hanns-Braun-
Str.
U
D.-Bonhoeffer-GS
Brix-pl.
Kornblumen-
Gothaallee
Koburg-allee
Westend-
Meiningen-allee
Heid-
Altenburg-Allee
Bolivar-
Ulmenallee
174
St.-Elisabeth Stift
Akazienallee
Nußbaumallee
Eichenallee
Jugend-werkhm.
Klinik d. FU
Nußbaumallee
Akazienallee
Wasserwerk Charlottenburg
Wasserturm
Spandauer-Damm-Br.
S
Klausener-pl.
Gardes-du-Corps-Str.
St.-Kamillus
WESTEND
Neufel

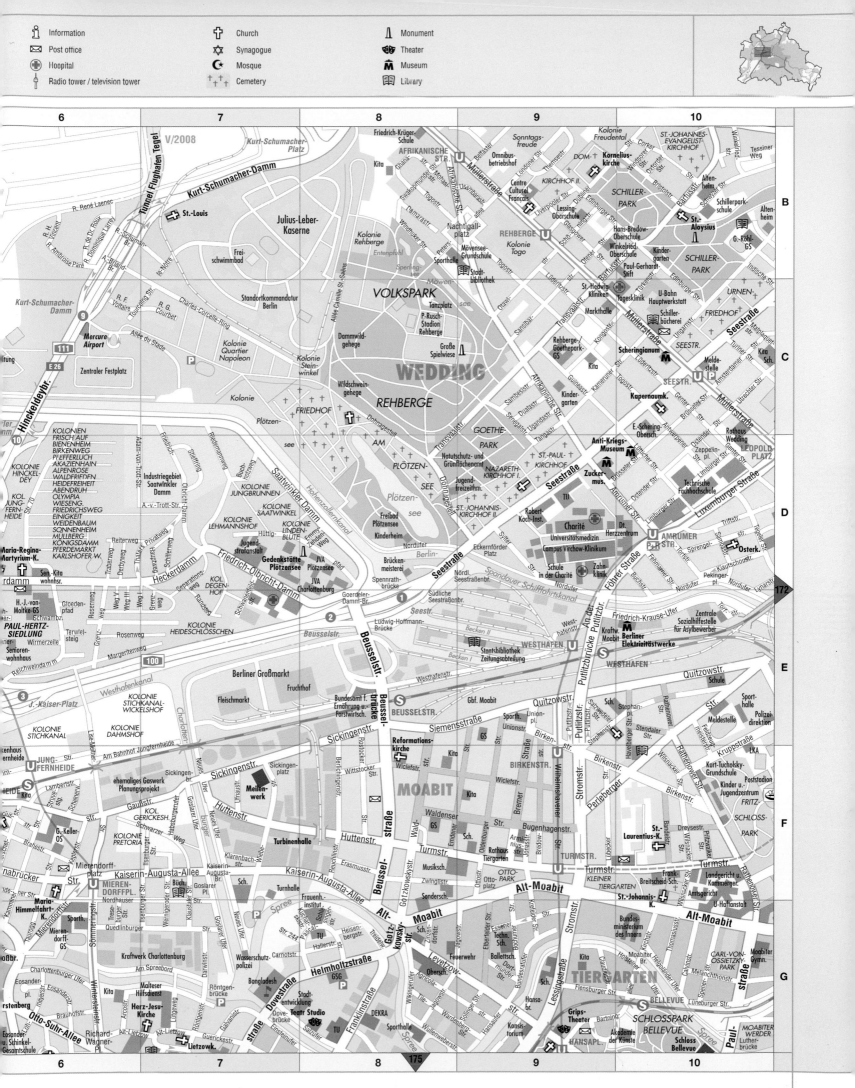

100	Motorway number	✈ Airport	Ⓢ S-Bahn station	Ⓟ Car park
1	Federal road number	🚉 Central station	Ⓤ U-Bahn station	Stadium
15	Motorway exit number	ICE/IC/EC Station for express trains	🚌 Bus terminal	Trade fair
➤	One-way street	DB Station for intercity railway transportation	P+R Park + Ride	Embassy

Index entries refer to both the maps and the picture section of this book. After each entry, page numbers and map references follow in bold print. Next comes the page reference to the picture section, and lastly there are Internet addresses for quick and easy access to current information for the sights featured in this book. Most entries in the picture section can also be found in the map section, which offers many additional tips for visitors.

From left to right: The Neue Nationalgalerie by Ludwig Mies van der Rohe; Schaubühne on Lehniner Platz; café and organic market in Prenzlauer Berg; the Konzerthaus in Gendarmenmarkt becomes a backdrop for open-air concerts in summer.

Picture Credits

MONACO BOOKS is an imprint of Verlag Wolfgang Kunth
© Verlag Wolfgang Kunth GmbH & Co.KG, Munich, 2009

© Cartography: GeoGraphic Publishers GmbH & Co. KG
Representation of terrain MHM ® Copyright © Digital Wisdom, Inc.

Text: Gisela Buddée
Translation: Sylvia Goulding
Editor: Kevin White for bookwise Medienproduktion GmbH, Munich

For distribution please contact:
Monaco Books
c/o Verlag Wolfgang Kunth, Königinstr. 11
80539 München, Germany
Tel: +49 / 89/ 45 80 20 23
Fax: +49 / 89/ 45 80 20 21
info@kunth-verlag.de
www.monacobooks.com
www.kunth-verlag.de

Printed in Slovakia